Cambridge Elements

Elements in Magic
edited by
Marion Gibson
University of Exeter

THE DONKEY KING

Asinine Symbology in Ancient and Medieval Magic

Emily Selove
University of Exeter

CAMBRIDGE
UNIVERSITY PRESS

CAMBRIDGE
UNIVERSITY PRESS

Shaftesbury Road, Cambridge CB2 8EA, United Kingdom

One Liberty Plaza, 20th Floor, New York, NY 10006, USA

477 Williamstown Road, Port Melbourne, VIC 3207, Australia

314–321, 3rd Floor, Plot 3, Splendor Forum, Jasola District Centre, New Delhi – 110025, India

103 Penang Road, #05–06/07, Visioncrest Commercial, Singapore 238467

Cambridge University Press is part of Cambridge University Press & Assessment, a department of the University of Cambridge.

We share the University's mission to contribute to society through the pursuit of education, learning and research at the highest international levels of excellence.

www.cambridge.org
Information on this title: www.cambridge.org/9781009462549

DOI: 10.1017/9781009076234

First published 2023

A catalogue record for this publication is available from the British Library.

ISBN 978-1-009-46254-9 Hardback
ISBN 978-1-009-07493-3 Paperback
ISSN 2732-4087 (online)
ISSN 2732-4079 (print)

The Donkey King

Asinine Symbology in Ancient and Medieval Magic

Elements in Magic

DOI: 10.1017/9781009076234
First published online: November 2023

Emily Selove
University of Exeter

Author for correspondence: Emily Selove, e.selove@exeter.ac.uk

Abstract: The thirteenth-century Arabic grimoire, al-Sakkākī's *Kitāb al-Shāmil* (*Book of the Complete*), provides numerous methods of contacting jinn. The first such jinn described, Abū Isrā'īl Būzayn ibn Sulaymān, arrives with a donkey. In the course of offering an explanation for his ritual, this Element reveals the double-sided nature of asinine symbology and explains why this animal has served as the companion of both demons and prophets. Focusing on two nodes of donkey symbology – the phallus and the bray – it reveals a *coincidentia oppositorum* in a deceptively humble and comic animal form. Thus the donkey, bearer of a demonic voice and of a phallus symbolic of base materiality, also represents transcendence of the material and protection from the demonic. In addition to Arabic literature and occult rituals, the Element refers to evidence from the ancient Near East, Egypt, and Greece, as well as to medieval Jewish and Christian texts.

Keywords: Arabic, donkey, magic, microcosm, occult, phallus

ISBNs: 9781009462549 (HB), 9781009074933 (PB), 9781009076234 (OC)
ISSNs: 2732-4087 (online), 2732-4079 (print)

Contents

1 Introduction: The Complete Donkey

Der Leser war also gewarnt. Wer mit dem Esel nichts zu tun haben wollte, hätte dieses Buch gar nicht erst aufschlagen sollen.

"The reader has been warned: if you didn't want anything to do with donkeys, you shouldn't have opened this book in the first place." Martin Vogel, *Onos Lyras*, 16

To start with the lowliest, most obscene, and abject material and to delve into it so deeply that one emerges at last into the loftiest reaches of heaven may seem a strange approach to modern readers. But it is a method well suited to the interpretation of medieval Arabic literature, where we begin our asinine journey. For this is a literature that makes paradox, ambiguity, and the coincidence of opposites its constant theme.[1]

This is a study of the magical significance of the donkey, using medieval Arabic literature as the centerpiece of a discussion that will touch on the development of the figure through ancient Egypt, Greece, and Rome, through the medieval Jewish, Christian, and Muslim worlds, and on into early modern Europe. By analyzing the use of the body parts of donkeys, as well as the invocation of demons, spirits, or gods who take the form of donkeys, it will show that in magical literatures across a vast range of time and space, the donkey has occupied a strangely liminal position. By focusing on his phallic associations on the one hand and on his ominous voice on the other, we will discover that the donkey has an unusually clear view into the world of the unseen and can consequently serve as a medium, an apotropaic presence, a holy fool, and a mirror to mankind.

I am a scholar of medieval Arabic literature, and much of my previous work has dealt with sympotic (banquet) literature, and specifically with the party-crashing character, or the uninvited guest. But my recent research focuses on magical texts, and specifically on a thirteenth-century Arabic grimoire, the *Kitāb al-Shāmil* (*Book of the Complete*) of Sirāj al-Dīn al-Sakkākī.[2] Though my focus is on medieval Arabic texts, I tend to read these in dialogue with ancient Greek and Roman as well as medieval and Renaissance European literatures. I have found the hub of these seemingly disparate (but actually intimately connected) research interests in the figure of the donkey. The donkey is the ragged, long-eared party-crasher on the gravest of philosophical and theological pursuits.

The first reaction upon hearing the word "donkey" is to laugh; similarly, the first reaction upon hearing the words "party-crasher" is to laugh. But the donkey and the party-crasher both present a deceptively simple comic appearance that

[1] See Bauer, *Ambiguity*, and Ahmed, *What Is Islam?*

[2] Al-Sakkākī, *Kitāb al-Shāmil wa-baḥr al-kāmil*, whose edition, translation, and analysis was the subject of the Leverhulme Trust's "Sorcerer's Handbook Project: Medieval Arabic Magic in Context," 2019–22.

hides a deep and powerful symbolic resonance. Like the divinity who arrives at your doorstep disguised as a beggar, these characters are microcosms who join the high and the low, the sacred and the profane, the obscene and the sublime, into a single presence.

The accumulated significances around the donkey are ancient and share a remarkably widespread afterlife through much of Europe and the Middle East. These regions are the focus of this Element, which makes occasional tentative forays farther afield. I touch on the symbolic relationship between donkeys and other animals such as snakes, pigs, gazelles, roosters, and hoopoe birds, but I do not attempt to delve too deeply into the symbolism of mules or (God forbid!) horses. Asinine symbology alone provides more than enough material for one volume because everywhere I look when studying religion, literature, history, philosophy, and magic, I find the humble donkey.

This is a study of the use of donkeys – their image, name, and body – in magic, and an explanation of the web of symbolic associations that lie behind these usages. Obviously these associations are linked to the historical role donkeys have played in human society, for donkeys are among our most ancient animal companions; they were likely domesticated in East Africa around 5000 BCE, 3,000 years before the horse.[3] Their symbolic significance extends far beyond the magical into literary and artistic representations. Animal husbandry, literature, and art are not the focus of this present examination of the occult, but for a brief, accessible overview of many of these subjects, I recommend Jill Bough's *Donkey*.[4] There are far too many literary or novelistic treatments of donkeys to mention, but Richard Bulliet's *The One-Donkey Solution: A Satire* is the closest to our context. Andy Merrifield's *The Wisdom of Donkeys* reflects on many relevant works of literature and philosophy in the course of a personal account about traveling with a donkey through France. Nearer to our purpose is Nuccio Ordine's dizzying analysis of the ass as a symbol of holy foolishness and *coincidentia oppositorum* in the work of sixteenth-century philosopher and mystic Giordano Bruno.[5] Martin Vogel's *Onos Lyras: Der Esel mit der Leier* touches on most of the topics covered in this Element, all in the course of

[3] Todd, Tonasso-Calvière, Chauvey, et al., "Genomic History and Global Expansion of Domestic Donkeys," 1172.

[4] Tobias and Morrison also provide a breezy, popularizing account of all things asinine in *Donkey: The Mystique of Equus Asinus*, which includes many full-colored photographs of donkeys and their artistic representations.

[5] Ordine, *La Cabala Dell'Asino: Asinità e Conoscenza Giordano Bruno*: the analysis focuses almost entirely on the writings of Bruno himself, and does not mention the Islamic or Arabic treatments of this subject, but provides a very condensed history of the ancient and medieval symbolism of the ass in "Myths, Fables, Tales: The 'Asinine' Materials," 9–18, the notes for which furthermore provide numerous references to primary and secondary sources. The work was translated by Baranski and Saiber as *Giordano Bruno and the Philosophy of the Ass*. Also see

advancing his charming but rather extreme argument, that the God of the Bible was a donkey god and the donkey himself is at the root of human culture.[6] I refer to a number of other useful studies throughout, notably Kathryn Smithies's *Introducing the Medieval Ass*, Richard Bulliet's *Hunters, Herders, and Hamburgers*, Kenneth Way's *Donkeys in the Biblical World*, Peter Mitchell's *The Donkey in Human History*, and Bassām 'Abd al-Wahhāb al-Jābī's *Akhbār al-ḥamīr fī-l-adab al-'Arabī* (*Accounts of Donkeys in Arabic Literature*), as well as many articles pertaining to donkeys in Greek, Latin, Egyptian, and Arabic literatures and beyond. When I stray outside my own area of expertise (medieval Arabic literature), I rely on the secondary scholarship and readily available translations, and I therefore apologize in advance for trampling on so many others' fields of expertise.

We will begin our exploration of *Asinità* (as Bruno calls it) with the thirteenth-century Arabic grimoire that lies at the crossroads of the civilizations that are the focus of this Element. We will see that the donkey appears in this handbook of magic as a powerful symbol of the unseen realm, used in both curses and love spells, as well as in the production of terrifying, sleep-disturbing visions. Because I argue that we can understand these varied and often contradictory uses as concentrated around two key features of the donkey – his phallus and his voice – I generally refer to the donkey as "he," given the symbolic weight of the male generative organ in this study. We should note, however, that one of the most famous and significant donkeys in human history, Balaam's biblical ass, was a jenny.

Sirāj al-Dīn al-Sakkākī's thirteenth-century Arabic grimoire (the *Kitāb al-Shāmil* or *Book of the Complete*) strives to contain all of the magical operations that a complete practitioner of the occult arts might wish to employ, ranging from curses and demonic contracts to rituals of planetary ascent and protective uses of the holy texts. It draws from ancient Greek sources, includes chapters on the tantric rituals of India as well as on magical uses of Hebrew liturgy, and contains many ancient remnants of Zoroastrian, Babylonian, and Egyptian magic, which, as in most medieval grimoires, appear in a form so corrupted that they are difficult to identify with confidence. Many of the texts that it reproduces went on to influence the occult traditions of medieval Europe: its "Volume of the Moon"

Silvia de Leon-Jones, "Ass, Asino Cillenico, and Cavallo Pegaseo," in *Giordano Bruno and the Kabbalah*, 109–117.

[6] He excuses his apparent exaggeration by saying that it is his way of overcompensating for the neglect that the history of donkeys in human culture has thus far received in the scholarship (Vogel, *Onos Lyras*, 527). Unsurprisingly, his thesis proved controversial, and even the kindest reviewer calls it "startling" and "provocative," and observes that "it is difficult to judge whether we have here a valid thesis or an obsession with the animal that crops up at every turn" (Frankel, "*Onos Lyras*," 117).

and "Volume of Venus" in particular were translated into Latin.[7] It is indeed, therefore, a complete book at the crossroads of the various times and places we will address in this Element, and a fitting place from which to begin our wide-ranging exploration of the magical donkey.

A significant proportion of this *Book of the Complete* deals with rituals used to contact the jinn, typically invisible creatures made of fire, who are featured in both the Qur'an and the hadith (accounts of the deeds and sayings of the prophet Muhammad). Jinn come in many varieties, practice many faiths, and take many forms, and they can be summoned for many magical purposes. In the *Book of the Complete*, they are often summoned with the intention of causing overwhelming lust in an intended victim. The first specific jinn that this grimoire describes arrives in the company of donkeys. We may ask why the jinn king takes this entourage, and how we can explain the troubling imagery that surrounds his ritual:

> On seals restricted to [particular] names of kings of the jinn. The first is a seal of Abū Isrā'īl Būzayn ibn Sulaymān, who is king of the donkeys. If you want to craft with it, clear out a house, sweep it, and sprinkle it with water, and spread it with fine carpets. When it is the time of the evening prayer, take care that the eyes of men are asleep, then get up and enter the house, and suffumigate it with aloeswood and costus, and put a glass vessel in the middle of the house, and cast into it something that I will explain to you afterwards. Let the goblet be of white glass, except that on the first night when there could be colours in it. Then gird yourself and draw the magic circle . . . Then you sit in the magic circle for seven, fourteen, or twenty-one nights, as you prefer, and recite the incantation on the first night – seven, fourteen, or twenty-one times – so that they may come to you on the first night, the middle night, or the seventh night.
>
> On the first night they bring you more than a hundred thousand, when they will come to you striking with their weapons all around the land. On the second night, they bring about a thousand, and on the third, three hundred, until the seventh night, on which they bring seven hundred thousand. When it is the time to bring the great king Abū Isrā'īl Būzayn ibn Sulaymān, you will see something like a mule and a donkey, and on their backs there will be different types of carpets and rugs in that house, and the dais of the king is put in place, and on its right, seventy thrones, and on its left, seventy thrones. Then Abū Isrā'īl arrives and is seated on the dais with his servants standing at its feet. And this is the sign of Abū Isrā'īl: that there will be many things like shadows and spectres to the point that the top will reach the roof of the house. Then open his mouth, and if he accepts, he will take your head into his mouth. Do not be afraid, for

[7] This is not to suggest that they were translated directly from Sakkākī's version, but that Sakkākī preserved a text in his compilation that definitely reached Europe by some route. See Saif, "A Preliminary Study," 27–28, on the Lunar Mansion chapter, and Ockenström, "The Deviance of Toz," on the book of Venus. Moreover, Arabo-Islamic jinn-summoning rituals like this one clearly also influenced medieval European Solomonic demon-summoning rituals. See Gordon, "Al-Sakkaki's Grimoire and Medieval European Books of Ritual Magic."

[fear] will destroy you; he is a Muslim and will not kill you. Then he will speak with you, and fulfil whatever you desire, so divulge your will, and he will reply. Then make the contract and the agreement with him . . .

If you want to learn this seal, make a seal of good quality steel, with a gemstone of it [as well], and let the stone be round without any corners, and engrave on it this engraving [as below]. And make the circle like a serpent with two heads, and in the middle, the seal of Solomon, fitting there exactly, neither too big nor too small. This is the seal which I mentioned; take care that it is done well.[8]

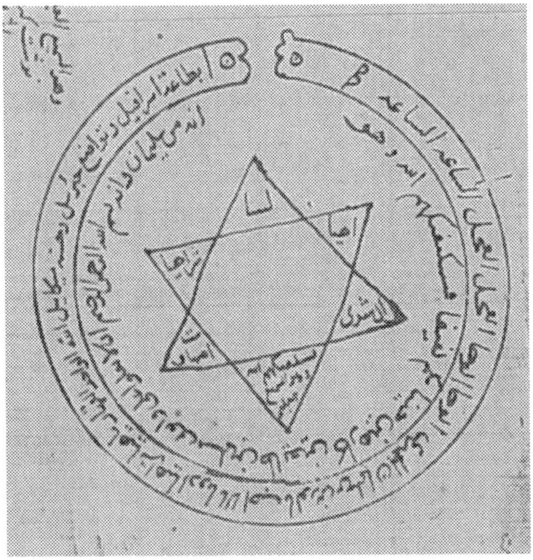

Figure 1 A seal of Solomon surrounded by snakes. On the outer circle, it reads: "With the obedience of Israfil, the modesty of Gabriel, and the goodness of Michael, God is One, All-Conquering, *I will be what I will be, the Lord* [in Hebrew], surely you must answer, O Būzayn son of Solomon the Donkey [King], Hie! Hie! Swiftly! Swiftly! Now! Now!" On the inner circle, it reads: "Lo! it is from Solomon, and lo! it is: In the name of Allah, the Beneficent, the Merciful; Exalt not yourselves against me, but come unto me as those who surrender."[9] The star itself is inscribed with the Hebrew phrase *I will be what I will be, the Almighty God of Hosts*, plus [*nomina barbara*] and "May God fulfil you, for He is the Hearing, the Knowing." Sirāj al-Dīn al-Sakkākī, *Kitāb al-Shāmil wa-baḥr al-kāmil*, "Cairo" manuscript, Juma al-Majid Cultural Centre, folio 117a.

[8] Sakkākī, *Kitāb al-Shāmil* ("Cairo" manuscript), 115b–117a. Unless otherwise stated in the bibliography, all translations are mine.

[9] Qur'an 27:30–31, translated by Marmaduke Pickthall.

A number of questions present themselves in this evocative passage, namely why is the donkey king the first and arguably most important jinn king presented in this manuscript? Why does his name associate him with Israel and with Solomon in particular? Why is he a Muslim but an ambiguously friendly/unfriendly being? Why the focus on his mouth? Why might we feel an urge to laugh at such a frightening and solemn spell merely because it mentions a donkey?

We are also struck by the "sign" of the donkey king – the shadows and specters piling up to the roof of the house. The jinn in general have the power to disturb human minds with their illusions and specters, perhaps especially in our sleep, but this is particularly true of Abū Isrāʾīl.[10] I would argue that this is because of his relationship with donkeys. An earlier chapter of the *Book of the Complete* tells us how to create "illusion," or *takhyīl*, a word whose etymological root, kh-y-l, is related both to the phantom images that haunt half-sleeping lovers (*khayāl*) and to horses (*khayl*). The word *tahkyīl* itself often refers not to a magical illusion, but to a poetical figure of speech whereby one creates a metaphorical likeness and then manipulates that likeness as if it were the true object of the verse: a kind of poetic voodoo doll.[11] The equine undertones of this word's root are not obvious or typically remarked upon, but are nevertheless notable given our context.

> The talisman of illusion. When the moon is in [the fifth] mansion, take the mud from a river running north, and make of it an idol of a [person] with his hands together, and with three heads, and the feet of a donkey, with a staff in his hand. And inscribe the first letter on his back, and the second [set of] letters on his chest, and suffumigate with the incense of the mansion. Say to it: "Excite the spirit of fantasy in this house, and make various frightful images appear!" Then bury it in the house. You will see various images and unsettling shapes.

Although this talisman does not specifically mention the jinn, the statue's donkey feet are a telltale sign used to identify jinn of otherwise human appearance.[12] A later chapter of this grimoire describes an operation performed with equine footwear, used to activate an invocation to disrupt sleep, and calling on the donkey king for this specific purpose:[13]

---

[10] See Jacobi, "The 'Khayāl' Motif" and Seybold, "The Earliest Demon Lover."

[11] See Van Gelder, "The Lamp and Its Mirror Image." Also see Hammond, "From Phantasia to Paronomasia," which links *takhyīl* to the Greek concept of *phantasia* as well as the *ṭayf al-khayāl*. I argue elsewhere that the *khayāl* (phantom image) of the jinn and its link both to the poetic figure of speech (*takhyīl*) and to the *ṭayf al-khayāl* (a dream visitation from the specter of a distant beloved), is central to the operative power of the sorcerer as depicted in the *Book of the Complete*. See Selove, "Dream Theory of Translation." Sakkākī, *Kitāb al-Shāmil* ("SOAS" manuscript), 38a–38b.

[12] El-Zein, *Islam, Arabs, and the Intelligent World of the Jinn*, 172n4.

[13] Sakkākī, *Kitāb al-Shāmil* ("Cairo" manuscript), 159b–160a. The donkey king is again invoked for this purpose on 173a.

> **On another** [method] to excite. Take a shoe from the left foot of a mule or a horse, with three holes, and mix it with the blood of a black chicken, and write the incantation and the seal upon it, and cast it on the fire, suffumigating it with blue bdellium until it grows red. This is the incantation: "I conjure you, O band of kings and demons, and O masters of sorcery and foul whispering, of the soldiers of Iblīs (Satan),[14] and the demon Danhash, by the words of Maymūn the Nubian, and Maymūn the Zengid, and Maymūn the Abyssinian, and Maymūn, Master of the Indian assistants, by the right of Kūzīn Shu'abād[15] Solomon the donkey, King of Abyssinia,[16] take and bind the sleep of [Name] with love of [Name], son of [Name]!"

This section is found in a short chapter devoted entirely to insomnia. The chapter's closing thought confirms the link between donkeys and terrifying, sleep-disturbing visions. Immediately following this chapter is another on hatred and division, and this new chapter opens with yet another donkey spell. So donkeys end and begin these adjacent chapters of dark and aggressive magic. The following quotation provides the closing lines of the insomnia chapter and continues on into the next chapter on hatred as described:[17]

> The master of the Hidden Laws said that you bury the head of a dead donkey in the house of the person you wish [to affect] and no person will sleep in that house so long as the head is buried thus.[18] This is one of the secrets of the hidden laws. This chapter is now complete, with praise to God, may He grant success.

Chapter Three on hatred, binding, sundering, and enmity in hatred and division.

> The Shaykh Sirāj al-Dīn Abū Ya'qūb al-Sakkākī said: If you want to start down this path, take a piece of black wax and form two images from it, one in the name of the hater and one in the name of his mother, in such a way that the [statues] are both hollow. Write this incantation and this seal on a donkey skin and on the robe belonging to the hater, or if that is not possible, then on a menstrual rag or some other cast-off, hateful, loathsome rag, and wrap the donkey skin and the rag all together, and put it inside the image representing the hater, and recite the incantation seven times, saying at the end: "Raise and cast enmity, hatred, dispute, ignorance, affliction, and battle between them, such that they will not marry, nor walk side by side, nor look upon one another except in enmity, division, shackles and adversity, and such that there will be no affection or harmony."

---

[14] On the ambiguous status of the Islamic Satan, see Section 2.

[15] Both the voweling and meaning of these words are not clear.

[16] This epithet is only ever applied to the jinn Maymūm elsewhere in this text, and its inclusion here may be the result of a scribal error.

[17] Sakkākī, *Kitāb al-Shāmil* ("Cairo" manuscript), 162b–163a.

[18] This may refer to the author of the "ninth-century Pseudo-Platonic *Kitāb al-nawāmīs* ('The Book of Sacred Secrets')" translated into Latin as the *Liber vaccae* (on which see Saif, "The Cows and the Bees," 1).

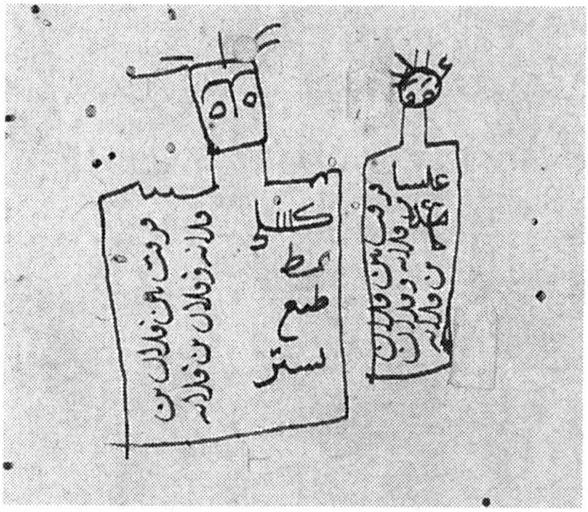

Figure 2 A spell of hatred to be inscribed on a donkey skin. The inscription reads: “I have divided between [Name] son of [Name] and [Name] son of [Name]” – SOAS library MS 46347, *Kitāb al-Shāmil wa-baḥr al-kāmil*, folio 179b

These spells provide a representative sample of the use of donkeys in this grimoire, which employs them most commonly for spells to cause hatred and affliction (a total of nine additional times to those already cited, once more especially by means of afflicting the enemy’s sleep). But *The Book of the Complete* also lists the donkey as one of the animals beloved to Venus and prescribes its milk as the key ingredient in a love spell: “Engrave [the seal] in the hour of Venus on Friday when the moon is in Taurus, then use it to stamp white sugar kneaded with donkey milk, and give this stamped [substance] as a drink to whoever interests you, and he will love you passionately.”[19, 20]

The use of donkeys for all of these purposes – to accompany conjured demons, to cause hatred, to induce insomnia, illusions, and nightmares, and to promote love and sexuality – is already found in the Greek Magical Papyri.[21] This diverse collection of magical texts from Greco-Roman Egypt, dating mainly from the first few centuries CE and written in Greek, Demotic, and

[19] Sakkākī, *Kitāb al-Shāmil* (“Cairo” manuscript), 16b.
[20] Sakkākī, *Kitāb al-Shāmil* (“Cairo” manuscript), 32a.
[21] See Lucarelli, “The Donkey in the Graeco-Egyptian Papyri,” which describes insomnia and nightmare spells on 92 and 94, a spell for sending dreams on 99 and for causing illusions on 101, hatred spells on 95 and 96, a donkey-riding goddess/demoness on 92 and 93, and love spells on 98 and 99. The texts described cover centuries of material starting in the second century BCE. Lucarelli considers the Set-donkey, prominently featured in Section 2 of this Element, to be at the root of these examples of donkey magic.

Coptic, describes magical uses for donkeys that remain stable for centuries. The uneven balance between donkey parts employed in curses and in love/protection spells also remains stable; in general, the negative connotations of donkeys continue to outweigh the positive throughout the history of asinine symbology. For example, the thirteenth-century Latin *Picatrix* (itself a translation of the Arabic *Ghāyat al-Ḥakīm*), recommends the use of donkey parts in eight spells of cursing and enmity, but only three of love and protection.[22] In general, the donkeys' negative symbolic qualities are their most apparent, while their opposite positive qualities are hidden, but arguably deeper, more mysterious, and therefore closer to the truth of creation.

The passage just cited refers to the "hidden laws" (*nawāmīs*) that govern creation. These are the divine secrets that lie behind the efficacy of the ingredients of magic spells.[23] They imply a network of significations hidden beneath the apparent image on the surface of things. Why does the form of the donkey hold these powerful and often contradictory meanings? Why do donkeys haunt our nightmares and lend their form to our monsters and demons? Why do they nevertheless appear to us in daily life as benign creatures, and why in our religions do they serve as the mounts of our prophets and our gods? Our quest for answers takes us first back to the ancient world.

2 The Ancient Donkey and His Afterlives

This section provides a brief overview of the ancient symbolism of the donkey and his medieval afterlives.[24] It focuses especially on the Egyptian god Set, who lies behind many of these associations, including the purported link between donkeys and Judaism, as well as the donkey's darker resonances in Christianity and Islam. I also introduce here the donkey as mount of prophets and gods in multiple religious traditions, thus setting the stage for the following sections, which will revisit these themes and explore them more deeply in relationship to the phallus and the bray.

---

[22] Book three of *Picatrix: A Medieval Treatise on Astral Magic*, edited by Attrell and Porreca. Saif, "From Ghāyat al-ḥakīm to Šams al-ma'ārif," explains, "The compendium known as Ghāyat al-ḥakīm (The Goal of the Sage, aka Picatrix), among the most influential of premodern grimoires, epitomizes the earliest tradition of natural magic in Islam. Usually associated with the astronomer and mathematician Maslama l-Mağrīṭī (d. ca. 398/1008), this erroneous attribution was made by Ibn Ḫaldūn (d. 808/1406) and others. Maribel Fierro convincingly identifies the author as the traditionist and occultist Maslama l-Qurṭubī (d. 353/964)," 299.

[23] Saif translates the word as "sacred secrets," and explains that the more common translation as "laws" derives from the etymological link to the Greek *nomoi* ("The Cows and the Bees," 1).

[24] Bough's "Donkeys in Human History, Mythology, and Religion" (*Donkey*, 45–75) provides illustrative photographs of many of the mythological and religious figures described in this section.

The Egyptian god Set was sometimes depicted with a donkey head.[25] The connection between Set and donkeys lies behind centuries of donkey magic. As Johnston notes, "It is probable that [the Setian] significance of the ass eventually became more broadly applied . . . so that it became a sort of all-purpose demonic animal, and its body parts became all-purpose amulets, *similia similibus*."[26] In the early Dynastic period (ca. 3100–2181 BCE), Set appears as an ambiguously friendly/unfriendly god, but he later came to represent evil, chaos, and foreignness.[27] Thus, he is usually depicted as a trickster and as the murderer of his brother Osiris (god of fertility and death). Set's donkey companions' loud brays and large penises were at odds with the ancient Egyptian sense of decorum.[28] Since donkeys were also the companions of the wild people of the desert, both they and Set himself came to stand for the chaos surrounding and threatening the civilization on the banks of the Nile. Donkeys would have been a common sight, however, all over Egypt, and an integral part of daily life, and in that homely, workaday light, they seem a strange symbol for uncanny foreignness.[29]

Both Set and his donkey companions are ambiguous beings, integral to and outside of Egyptian religious life. Thus, though they were "known for their evil doings and menacing abilities, their wickedness seems to have also served gods and humans in many occasions."[30] For example, donkeys were buried in ancient Egyptian tombs, facing eastward toward the sunrise; it may be that in Set's role as the slayer of Osiris (a god closely affiliated with the sun god Ra), Set himself gained a (negative) association with the sun.[31] This would explain the mysterious claim by Aelian, a third-century Roman author, that the ass is hated in Egypt because he "voids excrement after turning its back to the rising sun."[32] It is in any case typical of the symbolic donkey to contain both the thing (in this case, the sun) and its negation in one being. Thus we also see the donkey, symbol of Osiris's murderer, serving elsewhere as Osiris's doorkeeper, and as the mask of the sun at night.[33]

As Vandenbeusch explains, this asinine ambiguity is embodied in the word *hiw*, which means both snake and donkey, or sometimes, a hybrid snake–donkey creature. It also refers to the frightening noise that both animals make

[25] The most complete recent study of this association can be found in Love, "'Crum's Chicken."
[26] Johnston, "Defining the Dreadful," 385.
[27] See Turner, "Seth," which speculates that his ambiguous status arose from the troubled relationship between Upper and Lower Egypt.
[28] Mitchell, *The Donkey in Human History*, 54n50.
[29] Mitchell, *The Donkey in Human History*, 45 ff.
[30] Vandenbeusch, "Thinking and Writing 'Donkey,'" 138.
[31] Mitchell, *The Donkey in Human History*, 54.
[32] Aelian, *De Natura Animalium*, 10.28.
[33] Guilhou, "L'âne, portier de l'au-delà," 183.

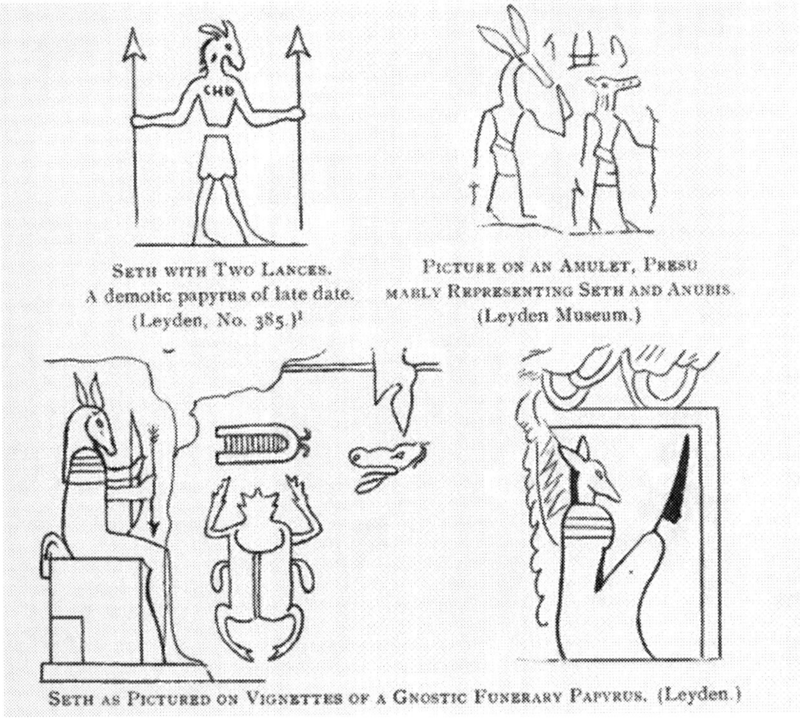

Figure 3 Pictures of donkey-headed Set, as reproduced in Carus, "Anubis, Set, and Christ, The Significance of the 'Spottcrucifix,'" 75

(the hiss and the bray).[34] Since donkeys were considered the natural enemy of snakes,[35] the term *hiw* therefore conveys duality embodied in one form: "the duality of two animals in total antagonism."[36] The Greeks identified the donkey-headed Set with the evil snake-headed giant Typhon, once again merging these two natural enemies, donkey and snake, into one being.[37] It is tempting to perceive a recipe in the thirteenth-century *'Uyūn al-ḥaqā'iq* ("Sources of truth") as an explosive collapsing of these opposites, resulting in a dragon-like creature: the text recommends burying black-eyed peas soaked in donkey blood in a place where donkeys urinate for three months, with the ultimate goal of creating a rooster-crested, winged snake called a *ṭalmūs*.[38]

---

[34] See Ward, "The Hiw-Ass," 25–26. [35] See Way, *Donkeys in the Biblical World*, 34–35, 58.

[36] Vandenbeusch, "Thinking and Writing 'Donkey,'" 142.

[37] Litwa describes several magical gemstones that depict Typhon with the head of a donkey and the legs of a snake in the section "Excursus: Seth–Yahweh in Spells and Gems," in the chapter "The Donkey Deity," *The Evil Creator*.

[38] Saif, "The Cows and the Bees," 30. Also see footnote 23 for this and other works on "sacred secrets."

It may be that the donkey's ability to kill venomous snakes with a sharp hoof lies at the very root of this animal's apotropaic powers, and the antagonism between donkey and snake plays out in the history of magic and medicine.[39] Set is depicted repelling snakes from the sacred barque of Ra in the Egyptian *Book of the Dead*.[40] The tractate Shabbat in the Babylonian Talmud writes that the fetus of the white donkey can be placed upon a snakebite for a cure.[41] The *Book of Secrets*, attributed to Albertus Magnus, recommends burning the lungs of an ass to rid the home of serpents.[42] It is likely that the compiler of this sixteenth-century text was drawing on an ancient source, such as Pliny the Elder's *Natural History*, which states that "all venomous creatures run away from an ass's burning lung."[43]

The ambiguity of the Setian *hiw*, however, shows that the donkey is not only protection against but the very symbol of the evil so archetypally represented in the figure of the serpent. Later religious traditions therefore associate the ass with Satan, and ancient Setian resonances lie behind this association. An eighth-century Coptic love spell, for example, depicts Satanic demons as the ass-headed Set.[44] Satanic donkey associations abound in the Middle Ages, and sometimes take a comic aspect, as in the following anecdote related by ninth-century Arabic prose master al-Jāḥiẓ:[45]

> Some ignoramus told a story about Satan entering the belly of a donkey once. That was because when Noah went on the ark, the donkey demurred out of stubbornness and ill temper, and Satan grabbed onto his tail. Others say he was actually in his belly, and when Noah said to the donkey, "Get in the ark, you damned thing!" and the donkey went in, Satan went with him, since he was in his belly. Later when Noah saw Satan in the ark, he said, "Who let you on the ship, Accursed One?!"
> "You ordered me in!" said Satan.
> "When did I order you in?" asked Noah.
> "When you said [to the donkey], 'Get in, you damned thing!,' for the only one damned there was me!"[46]

Here the donkey's negative traits of stubbornness and gluttony mark him as a vessel for the damned and as a fitting means by which to convey evil into the

[39] Vogel, *Onos Lyras*, 462. [40] Turner, "Seth," 106.

[41] See *Shabbat* 109b, translated by Steinsaltz in the *William Davidson Talmud* on Sefaria.org.

[42] Best and Brightman, *Book of Secrets*, 91. [43] Pliny, *Natural History*, 28.42.

[44] Grumach, "On the History of a Coptic Figura Magica." Also see Litwa, section "Excursus: Seth–Yahweh in Spells and Gems," in chapter "The Donkey Deity," in *The Evil Creator*, which provides several more examples.

[45] Al-Damīrī, *Ḥayāt al-ḥayawān al-kubrā*, 1:352, tells the story of a man who meets Satan on the road, and he is leading a donkey loaded with sins. Also see al-Jābī, *Akhbār al-ḥamīr*, 131, and Smithies, *Introducing the Medieval Ass*, 49.

[46] Al-Jāḥiẓ, *al-Ḥayawān*, 2:322.

postdiluvian world. We should note, however, the ambiguous status of Iblīs (Satan) in the Islamic context, for as we will see in coming sections, it mirrors the ambiguous status of the donkey. In some of the more sympathetic (mostly Sufi) versions of his tale, Iblīs's exile from the proximity of his creator is portrayed as the agonizing separation of the lover from the beloved. By tempting sinners into hell, he dutifully enacts his beloved creator's divine plan, of which he is just the instrument.[47]

In his study of the early Christian "evil creator" figure, Litwa paints another complicated picture of the relationship between God and the devil, and the donkey is in the center of this picture. Litwa shows that the ancient Egyptians had reason to conflate the sometimes frightening, desert-dwelling Yahweh with Set, and the resulting imagined donkey-headed Set–Yahweh god haunts polemics against Jews as well as early Christians (as we will see further). He goes on to show how some Christian groups, in criticizing both Jewish groups and rival Christians, themselves adopted the donkey-headed deity image to represent the Judaean god as chaotic and evil, and even as the father of the devil and the enemy of Christ.[48]

German musicologist Martin Vogel controversially argued that the God of the Bible was indeed originally a donkey god, and Jesus (rather than the devil) was "the Son of the Donkey God."[49] Given his love and respect for donkeys, Vogel did not mean his argument as an insult. He excited much criticism all the same, partly because of his dubious efforts to etymologically link the various names of God (e.g., Yahweh and Adonai) to words for donkeys or to the sounds that donkeys make (i.e., "hee-haw/hinham"). These sounds, he explains, were so loud and powerful that they could be used to call upon a deity.[50] Vogel also bases his argument on the fact that Exodus 13:13 forbids the ritual sacrifice of the donkey's firstborn, requiring that a lamb be used instead: "And every firstling of an ass thou shalt redeem with a lamb; and if thou wilt not redeem it, then thou shalt break his neck: and all the firstborn of man among thy children shalt thou redeem."[51] In glossing this verse, Vogel points out that the firstborn of man is mentioned in the same breath as the donkey, and he links the implied sacrifice to Jesus's crucifixion.[52] But it is unclear if Exodus 13:13's sacrificial

[47] As addressed further in what follows, this version of the Satan story is the theme of Awn's *Satan's Tragedy and Redemption*. See especially pages 85–86, which focus on Rūmī's *Mathnawī*, a collection of verse that features prominently in this Element.

[48] Litwa, "The Donkey Deity," and "The Father of the Devil," in *The Evil Creator*.

[49] Vogel, *Onos Lyras*, 273–284, 329–330, 527. Much of Vogel's argument throughout his hefty two-volume work relies on many tenuous etymological speculations, though he nevertheless provides a treasure trove of information.

[50] Vogel, *Onos Lyras*, 280, 322–323. [51] Exodus 13:13.

[52] Vogel, *Onos Lyras*, 285–286. Also see Bulliet, *Hunters, Herders, and Hamburgers*, 170, and Way, *Donkeys in the Biblical World*, 176 ff.

taboo stemmed from a revulsion from or respect for the donkey (as Vogel seems to think). The donkey is uniquely singled out in this verse as an unclean animal unfit for sacrifice, perhaps precisely in order to distinguish proper Jewish ritual from earlier ritual uses of the animal, either by non-Jews or by early Jews, before the new laws were codified.[53] This is to say, the donkey's unclean status may be a reaction to his once sacred position.

That the Jews do not eat the flesh of the pig or the donkey indicates that these animals are unclean; the same holds true in Islamic law, for donkey meat is not halal (and according to some hadith, the very presence of a donkey invalidates a prayer).[54] But there are vague hints that the flesh of the ancient donkey also held a sacred significance, again blurring the line between sacred and taboo. Aelian's *De Natura Animalium* provides a tantalizing suggestion of the early divine/healing powers of donkey flesh in a polytheistic context, and he concludes his observation with a groan-worthy pun: "It was this god (Serapis) who when Basilis the Cretan fell into a wasting disease, rid him of this terrible complaint by causing him to eat the flesh of an ass. And the result was in accordance with the name of the beast, for the god said that this treatment and remedy would be of ass-istance to him."[55] Orientalist William Robertson Smith (d. 1894) speculates that donkey flesh was protected by a sacred taboo among the ancient Arabs: "The wild ass was eaten by the Arabs, and must have been eaten with religious intentions, since its flesh was forbidden to his converts." But he later admits that, "As regards the eating of wild asses' flesh by the Arabs, I have not found evidence in Arabic literature that in the times before Mohammed it had any religious meaning."[56] It would be equally difficult to prove that it held any such significance to early Jewish peoples, though Vogel attempts to do exactly that.[57]

The Jewish people were, however, undoubtedly mocked by other ancient cultures as worshippers of the donkey, or of a Set-like donkey-headed god, an oft-repeated charge partly based on the similarity of the Greek word for Yahweh (*Iaō*) and the Egyptian word for donkey (*eiō* or *iō*).[58] This charge extended to

53 Way, *Donkeys in the Biblical World*, 177–181; Bulliet, *Hunters, Herders, and Hamburgers*, 153.

54 In a number of hadith, the prophet's wife ʿĀʾisha objects to the belief that if a woman passes in front of someone praying, this also invalidates the prayer, saying, "It is not good that you have made us (women) equal to dogs and donkeys!" and adding that the prophet Muhammad used to pray when she was in front of him. See *Sahīh al-Bukhārī*, book 8, chapter 108, 519.

55 In the original text, ὀνησιφόρον (onousiphoron) is the word translated here as "assistance," and ὀνησ (onous) is the word for "ass." Aelian refers here to Zeus–Serapis, a sun god of healing and fertility (*De Natura Animalium*, 10:35).

56 Smith, *Religion of the Semites*, 448–449. 57 Vogel, *Onos Lyras*, 289–290.

58 See "The Donkey Deity," in Litwa, *The Evil Creator*, which provides a history of this ancient accusation, especially in sections "Seth-Yahweh," and "The Ass God."

early Christians, as in the famous graffito depicting Christians worshiping a donkey-headed man crucified on a cross.[59] The second-century Christian writer Tertullian describes a picture of a man with a donkey head and donkey hoofs carrying a book, which he says was meant to represent God, though he is amused rather than offended by the portrayal.[60] The Jewish historian Flavius Josephus (d. ca. 100 CE) refutes these charges, stating that to the Jews, asses are merely beasts of burden to be beaten into submission.[61] The fact that he felt the need to say so, however, shows how urgently he wished to refute the charge of Jewish reverence for donkeys.

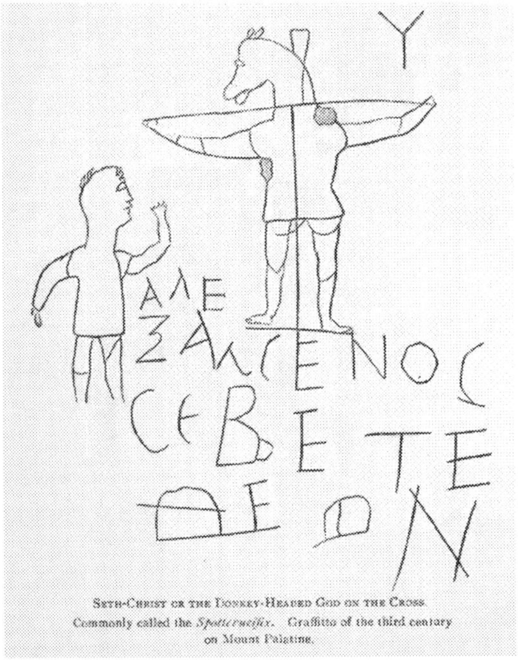

Seth-Christ or the Donkey-Headed God on the Cross.
Commonly called the *Spottcrucifix*. Graffito of the third century
on Mount Palatine.

Figure 4 Image of the donkey-headed god on the cross, as reproduced in Carus, "Anubis, Set, and Christ, the Significance of the 'Spottcrucifix,'" 95.

59 Bulliet, *Hunters, Herders, and Hamburgers*, 165. Litwa speculates on the origins of the association of the Jews with donkey worship, suggesting that Set was opposed to the other gods, as were the monotheistic Jews (section "The Alexamos Graffito" in chapter "The Donkey Deity," in *The Evil Creator*, 145–147). Also see Way, *Donkeys in the Biblical World*, 40.

60 Bulliet, *Hunters, Herders, and Hamburgers*, 164. The picture, he says, was carried by an apostate Jew. Also see Smith, *Jesus the Magician*, 62 and notes, which direct us to Josephus's *Against Apion* but also to Tacitus *Histories* 5.3 ff. (which states that Moses followed a herd of wild asses to find a spring when wandering in the desert).

61 Josephus, *Against Apion*, 2.7.

The connection of Jewish people to donkeys continued as a trope of mockery into the late antique and medieval period.[62] The Qur'an states, "The parable of those [who were] made to bear the Torah, then did not bear it, is that of an ass bearing books."[63] The medieval European literary and visual trope of the ass playing a harp mockingly depicts the animal as tone deaf and incapable, and therefore resembles the Qur'anic characterization of people who recite or profess to follow the Torah without honoring its laws as "donkeys bearing books" that they do not seem to understand. In medieval Christian Europe, the harp-playing ass came to represent the Jew as "the unbeliever who deliberately wishes to remain ignorant."[64] But even some Jewish writers symbolically use the donkey in this way, for the *Zohar*, a thirteenth-century mystical text produced in Iberia, calls those who understand only the literal and not the deeper meaning of the Torah "donkey-riders."[65] These symbolic uses of donkeys are apparently very ancient, for more than 2,000 years before the Qur'an referred mockingly to donkeys carrying books, a didactic Egyptian papyrus text asks, "Do you not recall the (fate of) the unskilled man? His name is not known. He is ever burdened [like an ass . . . carrying] in front of a scribe."[66]

Donkeys, however, bore not only holy texts on their backs, but holy men and even gods. They performed this service of divine and royal mount since the earliest records of human history. Donkeys' role as conveyer of kings is among their most ancient: archaeological records of their ritual sacrifice and burial confirm their royal symbolism in the ancient Near East.[67] At least in some contexts, it seems that ancient kings rode to war on a horse, but rode donkeys on benevolent errands.[68] Thus, though Christians came to associate the donkey that Jesus rode into Jerusalem with their savior's humility, it may

[62] Take for example these lines by the twelfth-century Anglo-Norman poet Phillippe de Thaon: "By the ass we understand/ The Jews by great reason. /The ass is foolish by nature . . . /Never will he depart from his ways" (translated by Smithies, *Introducing the Medieval Ass*, 52). Also see van Schaik, *The Harp in the Middle Ages*, 127.

[63] Q 62:5 as translated in Nasr et al., *The Study Qur'an*, 1370. Similarly, in Q 74:50–1, sinners flee on the day of judgment like startled asses. The donkey appears in a more complex light in Q 2:259, as explained in Section 3.

[64] Van Schaik, *The Harp in the Middle Ages*, 135.

[65] *Zohar*, 3.275b on www.sefaria.org/texts, a community translation project.

[66] Way, *Donkeys in the Biblical World*, 32, quoting Papyrus Lansing (BM 9994).

[67] Mitchell, *The Donkey in Human History*, 149, and Vogel, *Onos Lyras*, 287–288. Also see Mitchell, *The Donkey in Human History*, 95 ff., for an archaeological account of donkey burial and sacrifice in the ancient Near East, showing that donkeys had a special status. Wheeler details numerous instances of donkey burials and associates them especially with the Semitic Amorite people in *Animal Sacrifices and the Origins of Islam*, "Horse Sacrifices and Burials." Also see Way, "The Donkey in the Ancient Near East," in *Donkeys in the Biblical World*.

[68] Hanfmann, "The Donkey and the King"; Vogel, *Onos Lyras*, 292; Way, *Donkeys in the Biblical World*, 87 (the latter referring specifically to the Akkadian context).

be that his mount originally symbolized Christ's royalty, marking him as a king who rides in peace.[69]

Even gods ride donkeys: Dionysius, for example, prefers the ass as a mount. His and Hephaestus's donkey mounts were immortalized as the stars Asellus Borealis and Asellus Australis,[70] known as the *Onoi* in Greek and as *al-ḥimarayn* in Arabic ("the two donkeys"). These divine donkeys frightened the giants away with their powerful brays, or, according to an alternative account, carried Dionysius across a swamp and were subsequently awarded the gift of a human voice. One of these astral donkeys, according to this account, went on to lose a penis-size contest with Priapus and perished as a result.[71] These two donkeys in the heavens therefore represent the elevated/ sacred pole of bivalent asinine symbology, while also demonstrating the symbolic significance of the donkey voice and phallus.

We cannot overlook the comedy in these tales, however high they elevate the donkey, and as we will see in Section 3, the wine god Dionysius's mount symbolized not only divine power, but unbridled lasciviousness.[72] Similarly, in the case of the Hindu deities who ride donkeys, such as the goddess Shitala, their mounts represent their ability to cause or control disease.[73] Given their status as symbol of this disease, we should not overemphasize the dignity of the donkey's role as *vāhana* (divine vehicle) in that context.[74] The donkey was also the symbol and the mount of the malevolent Akkadian goddess Lamashtu, bringer of disease and torment, especially to pregnant women. In some cases, however, the donkey could be used to symbolically carry this malevolent deity away, and thus he provided an apotropaic function already in ancient Mesopotamia; as always, the two poles of donkey symbology tend to reverse, mirror, or blur into one another.[75, 76]

As was mentioned in the Introduction, devil, demons, and jinn not only ride on donkeys but sometimes walk on donkey hooves. A donkey hoof is listed among the identifying features of the Greek demoness Empousa, among other ancient demons of dangerously excessive female lust.[77] The seducing Onoskelis (Donkey-leg)

69 Smithies, *Introducing the Medieval Ass*, 44. 70 Ridpath, *Star Tales*, 58.

71 The contest with Priapus was "on a matter of physique" (as translated by Mary Grant) (*contendisse de natura*) (Hyginus, *Astronomica*, 2.23.2–3). This is repeated by Lactantius (*Institutiones Divinae*, 1.21.4).

72 Mitchell, *The Donkey in Human History*, 151.

73 Wirkud, "Study of Gadhegals in Maharashtra," 56.

74 The Gardabha, or donkey, is typically the mount of "impure beings" in this religious context. See Dallapiccola, "Vāhanas."

75 Johnston, "Defining the Dreadful," 377; Budge, *Amulets and Magic*, 97, 114–115; Chu et al., *Religion, Culture, and the Monstrous*, 146, 148; Lucarelli, "The Donkey in Graeco-Egyptian Papyri," 93.

76 Johnston, "Defining the Dreadful," 377, 386. Also see footnote 198.

77 Johnston, "Defining the Dreadful," 377–379.

demon of the first-century *Testament of Solomon* proclaims to have been born from an uncanny voice, evoking, perhaps, the chilling bray of the donkey.[78] The appearance of demons in the form of a donkey in the seventeenth-century compilation *The Lesser Key of Solomon* shows that Solomonic demon lore still features donkeys centuries later. See especially Samigina, or Gamigin, who appears either as a small horse or a donkey, and appropriately "speaketh with a hoarse voice." This spirit provides knowledge of damned souls, reminding us of the donkey's view on the underworld.[79] This is the quality that renders these animals the most suitable companion of prophets as well as demons.

The donkey was still playing a double role by the time of the arrival of Islam, serving as the mount of both good and evil. The prophet Muhammad performed his miraculous night journey from Mecca to Jerusalem on the back of a winged steed called al-Burāq, whom many hadith described as half donkey, half mule.[80] The prophet's earthly donkey, known variously as ʻUfayr or Yaʻfūr, was thought to have descended from a line of asses belonging to the prophets before him.[81] As we will see in sections to come, these donkeys provided their riders with a view on the unseen world. Some report that ʻUfayr, the final donkey in this prophetic line, mourned the death of his master, the "seal of the prophets," by jumping into a well and committing suicide.[82] The donkey, however, also conveys a number of false prophets and charlatans in the history of Islam, and even al-Dajjāl, the deceiving messiah of the apocalypse,[83] is described as the "imposter" who will "ride a whitish donkey, whose step is a mile long."[84]

78 McCown, *The Testament of Solomon*, 4:8. Johnston also mentions this demon in "Defining the Dreadful," 379. The Queen of Sheba herself has been described as having both donkey feet and jinn ancestry in some Ethiopian sources (Vogel, *Onos Lyras*, 462).

79 Overman, *The Illustrated Goetia*, 76.

80 "I was told that al-Ḥasan said that the apostle said:

> 'While I was sleeping in the Ḥījr Gabriel came and stirred me with his foot. I sat up but saw nothing and lay down again. He came a second time and stirred me with his foot. I sat up but saw nothing and lay down again. He came to me the third time and stirred me with his foot. I sat up and he took hold of my arm and I stood beside him and he brought me out to the door of the mosque and there was a white animal, half mule, half donkey, with wings on its sides with which it propelled its feet, putting down each forefoot at the limit of its sight and he mounted me on it.'" (Guillaume, *The Life of Muhammad*, 182)

See Ibn Hishām, *Al-Sīra al-nabawiyyah*, 2:48. Also see Paret, "al-Burāḳ."

81 They were possibly two different donkeys. The prophet was also the owner of a she-mule named Duldul with her own fascinating lore and symbolic afterlife, but in order to keep our focus on donkeys, I simply direct the reader to Marashi's "More than Beast" for further information.

82 Bulliet, *Hunters, Herders, and Hamburgers*, 172–173. Also see "Riding Beasts on a Divine Mission," and al-Damīrī, *Ḥayāt al-ḥayawān al-kubrā*, 1:357.

83 Bulliet, *Hunters, Herders, and Hamburgers*, 176, 190 ff. Also see Mitchell, *The Donkey in Human History*, 155 ff.

84 Sindawi, "The Donkey of the Prophet," 89. He is translating the version of the tale told by al-Shaykh al-Saduq in his tenth-century *Kamāl al-Dīn wa-tamām al-niʻma* (*Perfection of Religion*).

Ambiguity is at the root of asinine symbology, and the donkey stands at the confluence of good and evil, trickster and holy man. The donkey is the ancient companion of demons and supernatural beings, both high and low, and therefore a suitable companion for a "king of the jinn" such as the donkey king in the *Book of the Complete*. Given the fraught relationship between Judaism and donkeys, we can now guess why this donkey king might be called Abū Isrā'īl, Father Israel. We can also understand why he appears simultaneously as a pious being and a terrifying entity, evoked side by side with demons and children of Iblīs.

Like the donkey, Satan is an ambiguous being, whom, as previously described, some Sufi texts depict as a faithful servant of God, heartbroken in exile from his heavenly beloved.[85] Moreover, Islamic traditions have identified Iblīs both as a fallen angel and as a jinn.[86] This debate hinges in part on Satan's ability to experience lust and to mate and reproduce (which, some argue, is characteristic of the jinn but not of angels).[87] Perhaps Rūmī is thinking of Satan's ambiguous status as angel (made of light) or jinn (made of fire) when he writes, "Lustful desire makes the heart deaf and blind, so that an ass seems like Joseph, fire (like) light. Oh, many a one intoxicated with fire and seeking fire deems himself absolute light."[88] But though Rūmī may have been thinking of Satan, he was talking about the donkey, upon whose phallus a lustful woman died impaled, as described in Section 3.

3 The Phallus of the Donkey

Magicians have used donkey parts in spells intended to cause harm and enmity, but they have also used them to protect. They have furthermore used them in love, sex, and fertility magic. The donkey's ambiguous status as provider of both curse and charm, and their association with the phallus, links it to the Roman *fascinum*, a phallic image used to ward off the evil eye. The phallus ("the one-eyed willy") is the mirror of the eye, and both the phallus and the eye are simultaneously vulnerable and potent organs, both receiving and emitting wounding impulses, their image a *pharmakon*, at once poison and cure. In addition to these talismanic properties, the donkey's phallus marks him as the symbol of bodily lust, and he therefore comes to represent man's base, earthly existence in the physical realm.

---

85 This is the subject of Awn's *Satan's Tragedy and Redemption*. One is reminded of Carl Jung's essay on the Trickster figure, whom he describes as "both subhuman and superhuman, a bestial and divine being" and the "forerunner of the saviour," in part because of his propensity for suffering (Jung, "Trickster-Figure," 263).

86 A subject of debate: see Awn, *Satan's Tragedy and Redemption*, 26–33, and el-Zein, *Islam, Arabs, and the Intelligent World of the Jinn*, 44–47.

87 Awn, *Satan's Tragedy and Redemption*, 27–28, 32.

88 Rūmī, *Mathnawī*, vol. 5, line 1366.

But he also promises that this materiality can be transcended. By taking these two aspects together – the donkey as *fascinum* and as symbol of man's earthly nature – we can regard the phallus as one node of asinine symbolism, to be balanced out by his ominous voice, which is discussed in Section 4.

The very hieroglyphs for donkey and phallus were related, and unlike other animals, donkeys were depicted engaging in sex in Old Kingdom Egyptian art.[89] A simultaneously threatening and protective function for Set's phallus appears already in ancient Egyptian magic.[90] A New Kingdom Egyptian curse prays, "May a donkey violate him, may a donkey violate his wife."[91] In a spell preserved from 300 BCE, the magician is instructed to smear his head with donkey's blood and threaten his enemies with penetration with Set's phallus.[92] Set himself, as a representation of evil, is warded off with a phallus in *The Book of the Dead*: "Another spell for warding off the donkey [referring to Set] to be spoken by Osiris . . . 'O you bald back of the head, pierce Seth!'"[93] The Set donkey could furthermore be neutralized by "ritualised impaling."[94]

Donkey parts have also been used in love magic seemingly throughout human history. Donkey milk, which we saw employed in a love spell in the Introduction, is among the human race's longest-lived beauty products, famously favored by Cleopatra. Pliny lists "ointment made from ass's suet mixed with the fat of a gander" and "the right testicle of an ass drunk in wine in a suitable dose or attached to a bracelet, or the foam from the same creature after sex in a red rag and shut up in silver" for purposes of stimulating sexual desire.[95] Similar use of donkey parts can still be found in late medieval animal lore, as, for example, in the Arabic list of special properties (*khawāṣṣ*) provided by al-Damīrī (d. 1405), which advises that a donkey tail tied around the thigh acts as

---

89 Mitchell, *The Donkey in Human History*, 54n50; Vandenbeusch, "Thinking and Writing Donkey," 140.

90 Moreover, Set's testicles are referred to in healing incantations (see Riggs, *Ancient Egyptian Magic*, 127). We might possibly perceive an apotropaic function for the donkey phallus in ancient Zoroastrian texts as well, for the *Bundahishn*, a Pahlavi account of the Zoroastrian creation myth, states that the Three-Legged Donkey purifies waters from "contamination of the Evil Spirit" by urinating in the water. Its eyes also have an apotropaic power: "With its six eyes it strikes down and overcomes the worst and most troubling dangers" (*The Bundahišn: The Zoroastrian Book of Creation*, book 24, verses 10–19).

91 Way, *Donkeys in the Biblical World*, 35; Frankfurter, "The Perils of Love," 493.

92 Bulliet, *Hunters, Herders, and Hamburgers*, 167–169. In these pages, Bulliet furthermore guesses that Set's animal's tail is phallic, calls the game of pin-the-tail-on-the-donkey "unconsciously phallic," and outlines the Vedic Indian association of the donkey with the phallus.

93 See Mitchell, *The Donkey in Human History*, 55–56n54, referring to the version found in British Museum Papyrus EA 10793.

94 Love, "Crum's Chicken," 678.

95 Pliny, *Natural History*, 28.80. Also see Vogel, *Onos Lyras*, 202–203, and Ogden, *Magic, Witchcraft, and Ghosts*, 243, item 232.

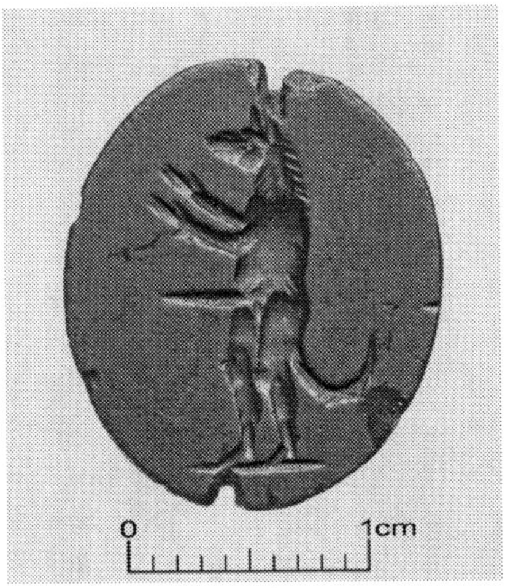

Figure 5 Magical gem found in Athens: Ithyphallic donkey on haematite AA. Seyrig.19, BnF, MMA-photo Serge Oboukhoff, BnF-CNRS-MSH Mondes

an aphrodisiac.[96] Indeed we find some evidence that donkey love magic persists in the modern age: Finnish sociologist Edvard Westermarck (d. 1939) reports a number of charms using donkeys' ears, brain, liver, and tongue, all of which allow a woman to secure her husband's romantic attentions.[97]

Because donkey symbolism is never simple and one-sided, however, we find at least one ancient claim that the Egyptians blame the ass for being "by nature opposed" to fertility.[98] It will come as no surprise that magic involving the sterile mule, in contrast to most donkey magic, tends to cause sterility, or to cure love-sickness, as in this entertaining example from the *Book of the Complete*:[99]

> **As for the those afflicted with desire** and love, its cure is found in this (astrological) house, for if the moon resides in this mansion, seek the pasture of a mule, and bury seven hairs in it, remembering their place, then . . . wallow in the pasture like a mule wallows, and draw near to the first hair, and extract it, and say: "I extract the spirit of love from [Name] son of [Name], and desire for her in my heart, just like I extract the hair!" And do this until you have finished with all seven hairs, and his feelings will fade with the permission of God, may He be exalted.

Aelian's accusation of sterility and the sterility of the donkeys' mulish offspring stand in contrast to the donkeys' more typical symbolic resonances of sexuality

[96] See al-Damīrī, *Ḥayāt al-ḥayawān al-kubrā*, 1:359.

[97] Westermarck, *Ritual and Belief in Morocco*, 2:288, 552.

[98] Aelian, *De Natura Animalium*, 10:28.

[99] Sakkākī, *Kitāb al-Shāmil* ("SOAS" manuscript), 46b. Also see Smithies, *Introducing the Medieval Ass*, 27, on the use of mule parts in infertility magic.

and fertility. In the Greco-Roman context, donkeys had a lascivious reputation and were depicted on vases as "ithyphallic" and sharing with satyrs an "aggressive and transgressive sexuality."[100] The fertility-promoting and simultaneously protective and threatening functions of phallic donkey magic put us in mind of the Roman garden god Priapus, who promoted fertile garden growth while threatening thieves and witches with his giant erection.[101] Donkeys were in fact sacrificed to Priapus in Lampsacus, where he was honored as a son of Hermes (another god associated with donkeys).[102] Other accounts record his father as Dionysius, who, as we have mentioned, rode a donkey, as did his companion Silenus, who either rode a donkey or walked on donkey hooves. (Priapus's antipathy for Silenus's donkey, who spoiled a sexual encounter with his raucous bray, is addressed in Section 4). Donkeys' status as companions of Silenus and Dionysius may in part be related to early Mediterranean winemakers' using them to carry grapes.[103] Bulliet directs our attention to a Hellenistic-era terracotta figurine depicting a man having sex with a donkey, who is carrying a basket full of grapes.[104] The image, it seems, at once represents an absurdly hedonistic pleasure and a sacred Dionysian symbol.

---

[100] Gregory, "Donkeys and the Equine Hierarchy," 204.

[101] For the donkey's association with Priapus, as well as with Silenus and Dionisius, see Krappe, "Apollon Onos," 225–228, and Vogel, *Onos Lyras*, 13–14. Also see Ordine, *La Cabala Dell'Asino*, 10, 209n9, which furthermore links the donkey to the symbol of water in this discussion, with reference to water's life-giving, fertility-enhancing powers (also see Vogel, 80 ff., 329–330). The importance of the Three-Legged Donkey for the protection, abundance, and purity of the ocean in the Zoroastrian creation myth confirms this link (*Bundhisn*, book 24). It is interesting to note that Westermarck reported a ceremony in Anjra, Morocco, occurring some 2,000 years after the time period described by Ordine, explicitly linking donkeys to rain:

> the women dress up a she-ass like a bride and take it to a spring, where an old woman of the company gives it water to drink . . . When the donkey has finished drinking, the old woman passes the vessel with whatever water is left in it to the other women, who fill their mouths from it and spit out the water on the donkey. This, I am told, has the same effect as pouring water over a saint, since the dressed-up donkey has the *baraka* of a bride. They then go with the animal to a watery and muddy place, which is believed to be haunted by *jnūn*.

Westermarck goes on to describe how the donkey and a woman are both thrown into the mud and drenched with water. This ritual is followed with prayers to bring rain" (*Ritual and Belief in Morocco*, 2:261–262). The donkey retains its saintly power in this ritual, as might be expected of an animal who has been the companion of prophets.

[102] See Lactantius, *Institutiones Divinae*, 1.21.4. Vogel links the donkey to Hermes, inventor of the lyre, thus rendering the donkey-with-a-lyre as a fundamentally Hermetic animal (*Onos Lyras*, 388–390). See Ordine, however, *La Cabala Dell'Asino*, 217n11, which casts doubt on some of the etymological speculation behind this argument.

[103] Also see Mitchell, *The Donkey in Human History*, 144 ff., on this association.

[104] Bulliet, *Hunters, Herders, and Hamburgers*, 177 ff. He directs our attention to *A History of Western Society*, 3rd edition, 157, for this image, but unfortunately it is not included in the many later editions of this work. He tells us that the figure is located in the National Archaeological Museum in Athens.

Priapus's role as protector of gardens may also help us understand the widespread use of donkey stones (*gadhegals*) in medieval Maharashtra, India. These stones depicted donkeys having sex with women, threatening similar sexual violations upon those (or the mothers of those) who would violate the terms of the land grant whose borders they protect. These *gadhegals* have also been read as a form of protection against the evil eye, which would further link the donkey to the apotropaic phallus.[105]

We find stories about people having sex with donkeys in a surprising range of cultural, symbolic, and philosophical contexts. In satires against early Christians (discussed in Section 2), the Christian God is parodied as an *onocoetes*, a word that may mean something like "donkey coitus," and which suggests a sexual union between man and god, or man and beast.[106] Stories of sex between humans and donkeys are typically liminal in import, hovering between divine and human, man and animal, high and low; they often appear on the surface to be no more than obscene jokes, but hide deeper meanings. It is perhaps in part the ability of the donkey to mate with a horse, creating the mule, that gives him this reputation for liminality in general and unnatural sex acts in particular, and that inspires, for example, fables of the onocentaur (half man, half donkey).[107] Tales in which humans have sex with donkeys often create, in effect, the image of an onocentaur – a beast with two backs, one of a human and one of an ass – depicting the dual nature of man as a simultaneously elevated and debased being. As we will see, however, such tales generally imply a "teaching moment" for the humans involved, and the donkey becomes thereby the herald of a moral revelation, a reformation, or even a transcendence of the human's earthly form. This is the donkey phallus as protection against evil on a profound cosmic scale.

The most famous example is found in Apuleius's *Golden Ass* (or *Metamorphoses*), in which the protagonist, Lucius, is transformed into a donkey, having ignorantly meddled with magic that he does not understand. After many misadventures, he meets a noble matron who, perhaps sensing his inner humanity, enjoys sex with Lucius the donkey.[108] When this secret pleasure is

---

[105] See Novetzke, "Traces of a Medieval Public," Wirkud, "Study of Gadhegals In Maharashtra," and Dalal et. al., "Gadhegals Discovered in District Raigad, Maharashtra."

[106] Litwa, section "Seth-Yahweh," in chapter "The Donkey Deity," *The Evil Creator*. Also see Smith, *Jesus the Magician*, 62 and notes.

[107] Smithies, *Introducing the Medieval Ass*, 28.

[108] Apuleius, *The Golden Ass*, X:22. Attributed to Lucian, the *Onos* is the Greek version on which this tale was possibly based. (On the scholarly debate about its authorship and dating, see Mason, "Greek and Latin Versions of the Ass-Story." Also see Schlam, *The "Metamorphoses" of Apuleius*, 22 ff.). The Greek version ends differently, with the woman rejecting Lucius after he turns into a man:

> When the night was now advanced and it was time to go to bed, I got up and stripped as though conferring a great favour and stood naked before her, imagining that I would please her still more by the contrast I formed with the ass. But when she saw that every

discovered, Lucius is tasked to perform the same act in order to punish a condemned murderess, but he refuses to pollute his body by commingling with this heartless criminal. In the very next chapter, by the grace of the goddess Isis, he is transformed back into a man and becomes a holy priest.

In analyzing this tale, Frangoulidis points out that Isis is the natural enemy of Set, murderer of her brother–husband Osiris, and that her followers therefore had an antipathy toward donkeys, even ritually slaughtering them by tossing them from a cliff.[109] In rescuing Lucius from his hateful donkey form, Isis therefore directs him away from the evil, destructive Setian (or, perhaps, Circean)[110] magic that his lustful curiosity had driven him to. According to this interpretation, his asinine character is reformed into that of a chaste practitioner of elevated, Isiac magic.[111]

Apuleius's tale is often read as a Neoplatonic parable depicting the ascent of man to a higher level of existence, an interpretation "reinforced by Platonic mythoi, in which souls corrupted by physical pleasure are said to be reborn in the form of animals, including the ass."[112] The ascent to true humanity cannot be achieved until after, like Lucius the ass, one overcomes the humiliating earthiness of this worldly life and its polluting pleasures.[113]

A Demotic Egyptian dream interpretation manual (ca. 100 CE), roughly contemporary with *The Golden Ass*, interprets dreams of a woman having sex with a donkey as a sign that "she will be punished for a grave sin," recalling the threatened punishment of the murderess in Apuleius's tale.[114] The symbolic logic behind punishing criminals in this fashion is derived from the donkey's status as symbol of humans in their fallen state. The donkey is "the animal match to women's own excessive carnality."[115] We also find the donkey used to parade criminals through the streets in multiple cultures, a form of humiliating

part of me was human, she spat at me and said, "Get to blazes away from me and my house; don't sleep anywhere near me." When I asked what heinous offence I'd committed, she replied, "By heavens, I didn't love you but the ass in you and he was the one I slept with, not you. I thought that, if nothing else, you would still have kept trailing around with you that mighty symbol of the ass. But you have come to me transformed from that handsome, useful creature into a monkey." (Lucian, *Soloecista*, 143)

[109] Frangoulidis, *Witches, Isis and Narrative*, 170, citing Plutarch, *De Iside et Osiride*, 362 e–f.

[110] Schlam, *The "Metamorphoses" of Apuleius*, 15, 68. Circe is, of course, the witch who transformed Odysseus's companions into pigs, in much the same way that Lucius was transformed into a donkey.

[111] Frangoulidis, *Witches, Isis and Narrative*, 169–174. DeFilippo explains how this dichotomy is interpreted in Platonic terms in "Curiositas and the Platonism of Apuleius's *Golden Ass*," 483 ff.

[112] Schlam, *The "Metamorphoses" of Apuleius*, 15–17.

[113] DeFilippo, "Curiositas and the Platonism of Apuleius' *Golden Ass*," 473–474.

[114] Frangoulidis, *Witches, Isis and Narrative*, 160.

[115] Frankfurter, "The Perils of Love," 493.

punishment that again uses the ass to symbolize the base condition into which the criminal has fallen.[116]

In a famous fifteenth-century sex manual by al-Nafzāwī, *al-Rawḍ al-ʿāṭir* (*The Perfumed Garden*), a seemingly lighthearted tale about a woman who has sex with a donkey makes a serious point not only about the lustful and tricky nature of women, but also about the importance of a man's obligation to sexually satisfy his wife; if he leaves her unsatisfied, it is playfully implied, she will naturally fall prey to her own debased nature and contrive to satisfy herself with the animal representation of this nature.[117] Smithies recounts similar stories found in the *Decameron* and *Libro de Buen Amor* (ca. 1300), all of which associate women's lust with donkeys,[118] an ancient symbolic link found, for example, in archaic Greek literature.[119] The Ketubot, a tractate from the Talmud dealing with marriage law, warns that if a woman drinks four cups of wine, she will try to have sex even with a donkey in the marketplace.[120] As we have seen, it is usually (but not always) women involved in these human–donkey trysts, which is to be expected given the widespread symbolic focus on the donkey's phallus.[121] But satires against men who engage in passive homosexual sex have also proposed the donkey as the only partner large enough to satisfy these inordinate lusts.[122]

---

116 Bulliet, *Hunters, Herders, and Hamburgers*, 169–170, and Bough, *Donkey*, 17. Also see Smithies, *Introducing the Medieval Ass*, 112, for a satirical picture of Napoleon in this posture.

117 Al-Nafzāwī, *al-Rawḍ al-ʿāṭir*, 131–132. Also see al-Jābī, *Akhbār al-ḥamīr*, 134, and al-Damīrī, *Ḥayāt al-ḥayawān al-kubrā*, 1:352–353, for another tale in which a donkey becomes the accomplice to a wife's infidelity.

118 Smithies, *Introducing the Medieval Ass*, 100. She appears unaware of the Arabic parallels to these tales, which are perhaps especially pertinent given the proven crossovers between *1001 Nights* and the *Decameron*, and the Muslim/Arabic literary influence in Spain.

119 Gregory, "Donkeys and the Equine Hierarchy," 204.

120 See *Ketubot* 65a, translated by Steinsaltz in the *William Davidson Talmud* on Sefaria.org.

121 Mystical treatments of Balaam's jenny provide an interesting counterexample, as discussed in Section 4. Another symbolically rich anecdote about a man having sex with a donkey is used in a ninth-century Zoroastrian refutation of Islam and Christianity to make a complex point about the problem of evil: "A man was seen having sex with an ass. 'Why are you committing this abomination?' they asked him. He said by way of excuse, 'Well it's my ass!'" This is used to mock the argument that because God is absolutely sovereign over all creation, He cannot be accused of committing violence against it. (My translation of the Latin translation of the Pahlavi Skand-Gumanik Vizar, rendered in Latin within Menasce's French translation because of its obscenity, *Une apologétique*, 143. This anecdote was brought to my attention by Kristo-Nagy, "Violent, Irrational, and Unjust God," 159n31).

Although we should take his reports with a grain of salt, given his complex allegiance to the sexual mores of his time (see Leck, "Westermarck's Morocco"), Westermarck records several interesting medical/magical benefits for men who have sex with donkeys in early twentieth-century Morocco, including the belief that this could cure gonorrhoea or cause the penis to grow larger (*Ritual and Belief in Morocco*, 2:289).

122 For example in *The Golden Ass* book 8, a *cinaedus* named Philebus purchases Lucius the ass for this very purpose. Blood, "*Sed illae puellae*," interprets this chapter as depicting "trans women rather than cinaedi" (163).

A most profound tale of sex between a donkey and a woman is told by Jalāl al-Dīn Rūmī, a famed thirteenth-century Persian Sufi poet. In his *Mathnawī*, he tells of a maid who enjoys having sex with a donkey by placing a gourd around the base of his penis, thus preventing it from entering too deeply. When her mistress witnesses her pleasure, she attempts the same trick, but not knowing to use the gourd, she is impaled and dies.[123] Rūmī explicitly associates the donkey with the beast-like soul (*al-nafs al-bahīmī*) in this parable and confirms that God gave "our fleshly soul the form of an ass." Although he then warns us "by God, by God, flee from the ass-like body!" the hero of this story, the maid, does not flee from the donkey.[124] Rather she uses it in an expert fashion, so that the donkey is wasting away from exhaustion in satisfying her desire. Moreover, by her skilled ministrations, the donkey is becoming civilized and has learned to make love like a man with "intelligence and design" (*ʿaql wa rasm*).[125] At the end of the tale, she warns that the mistress witnessed only the surface of her act – she saw only the penis and not the gourd. Or, as Mahdi Tourage argues in his dense Lacanian analysis of this poem, she mistook the phallus, symbol of esoteric secrets, for a fleshly penis, and her longing for God as longing for sex.[126]

"Have you ever seen one martyred for a donkey cock?" Rūmī asks sarcastically, warning us not to fall under the power of the bestial soul.[127] But the ill-fated mistress, not the donkey, embodies the bestial soul in this anecdote: she approaches him burning with lust, while the donkey enters her "politely" (*muaddab*), only playing his humble role in this parable of humanity.[128]

---

[123] Rūmī, *Mathnawī*, vol. 5, lines 1333–1405, pages 88–93. I use a mixture of Nicholson's and my own translations in this analysis, partly because Nicholson, out of modesty, renders any mention of sexual activity in Latin. An eighteenth-century Chinese novel *Guwang yan* (*Preposterous Worlds*) seems to marry the two tales from the *Perfumed Garden* and the *Mathnawī* – in this version, a sexually unsatisfied woman finds brief satisfaction with her trained donkey until her chair falls over, causing her to lose her grip on his penis. She then dies impaled upon it. It is possible some Confucian ethical moral is to be derived from this tale, but the interpretation of this often pornographic novel remains a subject of debate among scholars. See Ye, "Reading Bodies." I am grateful to Tianran Liu for drawing my attention to it and providing me with her own translation of the tale.

[124] Rūmī, *Mathnawī*, vol. 5, line 1395.

[125] Rūmī, *Mathnawī*, vol. 5, line 1345, translation mine.

[126] Tourage, *Rūmī and the Hermeneutics of Eroticism*, 68–98. Unfortunately, his analysis focuses on the phallus and says very little about the donkey himself.

[127] Rūmī, *Mathnawī*, vol. 5, line 1390, translation mine.

[128] Rūmī, Mathnawī, vol. 5, line 1386. I thank Christopher Soames for drawing my attention to the striking parallel found in sin-eating, a practice recorded mainly in eighteenth–nineteenth-century Wales in which a social outcast would accept food passed over a corpse along with the sins of the deceased in order to ease their passage into the afterlife (see Simpson and Roud, "Sin-Eating"). The comparison is apt because, like the donkey, the lowly scapegoat facilitates the purification of the sinner by indulging his own basic bodily desires (hunger, in this case). As discussed in footnote 198, the donkey has played the role of the scapegoat since the time of the ancient Hittites. This role is likely also at play in the animal's symbolic relationship to Jesus.

Meanwhile, it is implied that the maid's masterful interaction with the donkey was helping her overcome and reform the baseness that it represented. Just so, Apuleius's Lucius could learn to become a holy man only by engaging with the earthly realm in the body of an ass and learning from the experience. As Rūmī puts it elsewhere in his *Mathnawī* (here referring to Jesus), "Because . . . intellect was ruling, and the ass (was) weak – the ass is made lean by a strong rider."[129] We are reminded of the prophet Muhammad's donkey, 'Ufayr/Ya'fūr, who similarly transcended his own base animal nature, for when the prophet asked him, "Ya'fūr, do you want a female [donkey?]," he said, "No."[130] (I will further address this donkey's use of human language in Section 4). The polite donkey who refrains from rampant sex represents the reformed and elevated human body in all of these tales.

Doostdar recounts a modern-day tale of sex with a donkey as an educational encounter with the unknown. A professional sorcerer in a suburb of Tehran revealed the follies of his youth to the author. In hopes of relieving his teenage lust, he used a book called *Nikāḥ al-Jinn* (*Sex with Jinn*) to summon a beautiful female jinn. Midway through their lovemaking, however, the jinn transformed into a donkey, and thus did he find himself achieving climax with an ass. We can see that the donkey's link to creatures of the unseen realm, which we have already traced back to man's most ancient civilizations, remains a reality today. Doostdar furthermore comments that such a tale simultaneously allows us to see this sorcerer as a buffoon and as a man of enormous knowledge and power, for we may laugh at his mishap while still marveling at his abilities.[131] It should come as no surprise that we find the image of the donkey at this intersection between laughter and fear and between comic anecdote and profound revelation. This experience served as a fitting lesson for a young and reckless magician not yet in control over his own lust. His shocking sex act with the donkey provided a salutary nudge in the direction of a higher path.

Tales of humans transformed into donkeys also abound, and obviously also depict the thin line between human and donkey, again using the animal to illustrate humanity's lower, lustful, sinful nature.[132] The Greek Magical Papyri supply a recipe for causing party guests to appear to have donkey heads, and one could argue that the unrefined behavior of a typical drunken partygoer renders him worthy

[129] Rūmī, *Mathnawī*, vol. 2, line 1859, 317.
[130] Al-Damīrī, *Ḥayāt al-ḥayawān al-kubrā*, 1:357.
[131] Doostdar, *Iranian Metaphysicals*, 68–69.
[132] An apocryphal new testament story (written in the fourth or fifth century CE in Aramaic and then translated into Arabic) tells the story of man transformed into a mule by jealous sorceresses. The man is saved by Mary, the holy and chaste opposite of the lustful witch (Bulliet, *Hunters, Herders, and Hamburgers*, 184–185).

of such a comic transformation.[133] A prophetic hadith warns that a person who lifts his head before prayer is over will have it turned into a donkey's, punishing lack of self-control in an appropriate fashion.[134] I need hardly mention the world-famous example of this theme in Shakespeare's *Midsummer Night's Dream*, in which the enchanted fairy queen falls in love with the boastful fool Bottom, whose head has similarly been transformed into an ass's.

In the *Malleus Maleficarum* (a fifteenth-century treatise on identifying and destroying witches), we find a Christian version of Apuleius's *Metamorphoses/ Golden Ass*.[135] But this tale of donkey transformation is told as a true story – a warning that sorceresses and demons indeed have the power to cause terrifying illusions. In this tale, a woman in a port city of Cyprus transforms a young sailor into a donkey, using him as her slave for a year. At last she is captured, punished, and compelled to restore him to his human form, when he proves himself human by participating in the Divine Service and honouring the Sacrament.[136] The *Malleus* in turn cites Augustine's *City of God*, where again, an evil sorceress transforms her victims into beasts of burden.[137] Although sexuality is not explicitly mentioned in the stories, it could be argued that the men's bodily urges lead to their downfall, since they are transformed by eating an enchanted egg in the case of the *Malleus* and enchanted cheese in *The City of God*. In the *Malleus*, the anecdote is included in the chapter on "Remedies for those from whom the Male Member has been Removed through the Magical Art and for the Instances when Humans are Transformed into Animals," so it obliquely links the donkey transformation story to sexuality and the phallus.

An Arabic fable featuring Juha, the famous trickster/fool of Middle Eastern folklore, transforms these profound tales of human sin and forgiveness into lighthearted humor. Juha's donkey is stolen by a thief who hides the animal and then stands in its place. When Juha finds the thief in the spot where he expected to find his ass, the thief claims that he was himself the donkey, his human form thus altered by sorcery as a punishment for disobeying his mother. Now that he has been restored to his rightful human condition, Juha is only too happy to release

[133] Lucarelli, "The Donkey in Graeco-Egyptian Papyri," 101. See Best and Brightman, *Book of Secrets*, 97–98, which also includes instructions for causing people to appear to have three heads, or the heads of asses.

[134] See al-Damīrī, *Ḥayāt al-ḥayawān al-kubrā*, 1:339, who goes on to compare this image with Qur'an verses that tells the story of a Jewish community who breached the Sabbath and were transformed into monkeys and pigs as punishment (2:65 and 7:163–166).

[135] Mackay, *Hammer of Witches*, 432n547.

[136] It attributes these transformations to sorcery of the "East," influenced, perhaps, by *1001 Nights*–style narratives of the same (Mackay, *Hammer of Witches*, Part II 166B–167C, 431–432).

[137] Augustine, *City of God*, 18:18, in a chapter pertaining to the illusions of sorcerers, worked with the aid of demons. Also see Bulliet, *Hunters, Herders, and Hamburgers*, 169, and Smithies, *Introducing the Medieval Ass*, 116.

him. The thief is then free to collect the real donkey and keep him for himself. When Juha later finds his stolen donkey for sale in the marketplace, he whispers in the animal's ear, "For shame! *Again* you have disobeyed your mother!"[138]

Donkeys are considered stupid and feature in tales of foolishness partly because they represent man's bestial nature; thus do we often see fools like Juha riding (sometimes backward) on a donkey. But like the donkeys themselves, "who have a look as if to say 'you call me an ass, but you're the real asses,'" donkey-riding fools appear in some tales as very wise fools indeed.[139] Sancho Panza, companion of Don Quixote, is a familiar example whom I will mention again. Juha himself appears in many fables as a wise fool or a clever trickster. Even the great magician Zhang Guolao, one of the eight immortals of Daoism, rides backward on a donkey; he is a wise fool of cosmic proportions. Again, these images imply that donkeys represent not only sin and foolishness, but the possibility to transcend our human faults, while a failure to recognize our own faults by projecting them onto the donkey is the true mark of foolishness. This is beautifully illustrated in a tale attributed to the fool Juha's Turkish counterpart, Nasreddin Hodja:

> One morning the Hodja mounted his donkey facing the rump and trotted off.
> "Hodja" some folks called after him, "You've mounted your donkey the wrong way!"
> "I'm sitting properly," the Hodja yelled back. "The donkey is facing the wrong way!"[140]

As this anecdote shows, humans need not turn outright into donkeys to display asinine characteristics. In medieval bestiaries of the Christian world, "the ass's varied traits – asinine, irrational, lustful – were projected onto human nature," and "animals provided lessons for humans by which they should live a morally correct life."[141] The same holds true of al-Jāḥiẓ's famous Arabic bestiary, *The Book of the Animal* (*Kitāb al-Ḥayawān*), which reports the following shocking tale of donkey and pig behavior, relating them both to human moral failings:

> [A man of learning] said, "Sometimes I saw more than twenty pigs force a male pig into a corner in a narrow pass, and then mount him one by one until they'd all had their way with him!"
> And this man as well as other learned people of discernment told me that they saw donkeys do something similar. They mentioned that this behaviour either arose from the effeminacy of their nature, or because they have got

138 From al-Jābī, *Akhbār al-ḥamīr*, 36. Also see Ibn al-Jawzī, *Akhbār al-Ḥamqā wa-l-mughaffalīn*, 185, which does not attribute the tale to the famous fool Juha.

139 Al-Jābī, *Akhbār al-ḥamīr*, 25.

140 Translated by Birant Sevil in Birant, *Nasreddin Hodja*, 77.

141 Smithies, *Introducing the Medieval Ass*, 11, 21.

> a glint in their eyes like that which is seen to overwhelm some fellows when they look at boys and young men.
>
> Such acts may also occur amongst storks and cranes, as well males and females mounting one another. Cases in which both the top and the bottom are male are found often amongst all animals, but amongst pigs and donkeys it is more widespread.[142]

His comparison of the donkey's lust to that of a man ogling a boy suggests a moral judgment of both man and donkey.[143] Linking the similarly ignoble pig to this discussion strengthens this impression. The moral condemnation comes across more strongly in Ibn al-Mubārak's medical compendium, *Commentary on the Epitome of Ibn al-Nafīs*, where, in warning against the harms of such sex acts among humans, he writes, "It is sufficient to say with regards to the repulsive nature of sex with young men that . . . there is no species in animals where the male has sex with another male except the donkey. So, one who likes having sex with young boys . . . has the nature of a donkey."[144]

These condemnations imply an invitation to reform oneself and to be morally and spiritually reborn. Thus, as we have seen, the donkey's association with the sinful body is not divorced from its more mysterious and sacred connotations. Like the physical body he represents, the donkey holds a powerful, natural source of wisdom and healing, whose expression is at once prior to and beyond conscious human rationality. And although the donkey appears in the Qur'an most notably as a symbol of ignorance ("donkey carrying tomes,"[145]) and of loud-mouthed braying,[146] he makes a much more mysterious and esoteric appearance in his role as symbol of the resurrected body in the following Qur'anic verse:

> (Take) the similitude of one who passed by a hamlet, all in ruins to its roofs. He said: "Oh! how shall Allah bring it (ever) to life, after (this) its death?" But Allah caused him to die for a hundred years, then raised him up (again).

[142] He adds, "As for male and female pigeons mounting one another, it is usually when there is competition between them" (al-Jāḥiẓ, *Kitāb al-Ḥayawān*, 4:51–52).

[143] The *Rasā'il* of the Ikhwān al-Ṣafā'(4:114–115) speak reprovingly of a sex addict in the following terms (I summarize rather than translate): this sex addict, they say, would enter a room decorated with pornographic images in the company of his slave boys and girls, drinking and playing with them, and looking at the images in order to help himself become aroused. He would then assail the boys from behind, and might even scream like a cat and bray like a donkey, continuing in this fashion even if the boy was repelled by his ugly behavior. Even in his dreams, the sex addict will see these images and may again scream like a cat and bray like a donkey in his sleep (with thanks to Geert Jan van Gelder for pointing this story out to me).

[144] Nahyan Fancy's translation from his presentation "Infertility in the Arabic Medical Commentaries, 1240–1520," citing Süleymaniye MS Haci Beşir Aga 509, fol. 217b ff. Smithies argues that because the twelfth-century nobleman William Longchamp was associated with the ass Brunellus (the paradigmatic stupid donkey of medieval Christian philosophy), it was implied that he had a taste for homosexual sex, precisely because the ass is associated with "unnatural" sex acts (*Introducing the Medieval Ass*, 106).

[145] Qur'an 62:5. [146] Qur'an 31:18–19.

> He said: "How long didst thou tarry (thus)?" He said: "(perhaps) a day or part of a day." He said: "Nay, thou hast tarried thus a hundred years; but look at thy food and thy drink; they show no signs of age; and look at thy donkey: and that We may make of thee a Sign unto the people Look further at the bones, how We bring them together and clothe them with flesh! When this was shown clearly to him he said: "I know that Allah hath power over all things."[147]

The unidentified doubter in this story (possibly Ezra [or 'Uzair]), who cannot fathom the miracle of resurrection, is here presented with proof of God's power over life and death.[148] This enigmatic verse describes the resurrection of a dead donkey and of the man himself, who wakes up next to his donkey's decomposed corpse, to find the food that he had with him miraculously fresh, and to see the donkey restored before his eyes. According to a famous esoteric interpretation of the Holy Text, the *Tafsīr Ibn 'Arabī*, the drinks (milk and wine) that the man had with him represent useful knowledge, love/desire, and gnostic wisdom, "for wisdom is a secret treasure of every soul."[149] The donkey, meanwhile, represents the body pre-resurrection – both literal bodily resurrection, and figurative spiritual resurrection of one who was veiled in base matter, but who then gained wisdom and was spiritually reborn. The donkey is therefore the body of man in his lowest form, but with the promise of transcendence. In effect, the donkey plays the same role in this Qur'anic verse as he does in the philosophical-comical stories about people having sex with donkeys. In both cases, the donkey represents the base matter of man, but also the illustrative example which leads to his transformation.[150]

We might also read Christs's entrance to Jerusalem on the back of the donkey in this light, since Christ was also destined to die and to be resurrected, and

147 Yusuf Ali's translation of Qur'an 2:259.

148 'Uzair is a controversial figure described by Qur'an 9:30 as the "son of God" according to the Jewish people. He is not always identified as the prophet Ezra, and is sometimes depicted in a negative light, as, for example, a doubter of God's power. See Lazarus, "'Uzayr."

149 Ibn 'Arabī [attributed], *Tafsīr*, 92–93. Although attributed to the famous Ibn 'Arabī, this commentary is generally considered to have been written by the fourteenth-century Sufi Scholar Shaykh 'Abd ar-Razzāq al-Kashīnī.

150 Also see al-Damīrī, *Ḥayāt al-ḥayawān al-kubrā*, which tells the story of a donkey who dies on the road and who is brought back to life in response to the pious prayers of his owner. In the following anecdote, al-Damīrī relates that Abraham contemplated the decomposing corpse of a donkey, eaten by many animals on the beach, and wondered how there could be bodily resurrection. This is followed by an extended version of the Ezra donkey resurrection tale (except now it is Jeremiah's donkey, in the course of a missionary visit to the children of Israel [1:342–346]). See also al-Jābī, *Akhbār al-ḥamīr*, 109, 125. We find an odd echo of this image of the donkey as a human corpse in a tale from modern-day (2014) Tibet. A resident of Yagra relates that the local fairies like to imitate the actions of their human neighbors. When these beings witnessed the cremation of a deceased human, they "burned a donkey, thinking that was what they were supposed to do. But this was wrong, and it made their village visible" (Chu et al., *Religion, Culture, and the Monstrous*, 109).

thereby to redeem man from his lower nature.[151] This is no doubt why St. Francis called his own body "brother ass" before afflicting it with scourges. Saint Foy, of third-century France, was credited with repeatedly reviving dead donkeys, an act that accounted for four of her five miracles.[152] We can assume in these Christian contexts that the link between Jesus and donkeys is at play, and that these miracles therefore demonstrate the wonders of resurrection, literal and metaphorical. The donkey again represents the body before it is redeemed by Christ in a thirteenth-century English bestiary that interprets Exodus 13:13, "but the firstling of an ass thou shalt redeem with a lamb," as meaning that the donkey as "an unclean animal and symbolic of the worldly, represented the beginning of a life of lechery unless remitted to Christ."[153] According to thirteenth-century Flemish theologian Thomas of Cantimpre, the ass is melancholy for "on its shoulders it carries the marks of Christ's cross."[154] Vogel goes a step farther, insisting that the donkey's dark shoulder stripe is the very origin of this Christian symbol of suffering and rebirth.[155]

The association between the donkey and bodily resurrection forms the centerpiece of sixteenth-century Italian occult philosopher Giordano Bruno's obsession with asinine symbology. The donkey represents to him an aspect of Mercury as psychopomp and agent of metempsychosis, and the resurrection of the ass Onorio holds for him all the secrets of creation.[156] For when the donkey falls to his death, reaching for a bit of thistle on a precarious cliffside, he says, "Bereft of my corporeal prison, I became a limbless, wandering spirit; I came to consider how, in terms of my spiritual essence, I was no different in genus nor in species from all the other spirits . . . all spirits are of the Amphitrite of one spirit, and to that they all return."[157] Bruno interprets the donkey as a symbol of the fallen body redeemed in Luke 14:5: "Which of you shall have an ass or an ox fallen into a pit, and will not straightway pull him out on the sabbath day?"[158] According to Bruno's esoteric reading of this verse, "no good man ever resists coming to extricate the ass or ox from the well into which it has fallen . . .

[151] For a complete exploration of the numerous reenactments of Christ's entrance to Jerusalem, whether they were performed on a donkey, a palmesel (donkey replica), or white horse, with all the subtle spiritual and political symbolism entailed, see Harris, *Christ on a Donkey*.

[152] Smithies, *Introducing the Medieval Ass*, 54–55.

[153] See Smithies, *Introducing the Medieval Ass*, 50, referring to manuscript Bodley 764 in Oxford's Bodleian Library. See Way *Donkeys in the Biblical World*, 177–181, for the wider context of the redemption of the ass. Also see Krappe, "Apollon Onos," 232.

[154] Smithies, *Introducing the Medieval Ass*, 22–23. [155] Vogel, *Onos Lyras*, 295–299.

[156] De Leon-Jones, "Ass, Asino Cillenico, and Cavallo Pegaseo," in *Giordano Bruno and the Kabbalah*.

[157] Bruno, *The Cabala of Pegasus*, 54. The Amphitrite, or Goddess of the Sea, here represents the "source and origin of all things" (de Leon-Jones, *Giordano Bruno and the Kabbalah*, 117).

[158] King James translation. Jesus asks this rhetorical question after healing a man on the Sabbath, responding to the Pharisees' doubts about the permissibility of the act.

Behold, then, how the redeemed, worthy, desirable, well-managed, chastened, advised, corrected, liberated, and, finally, pre-destined populace is signified by the ass and is called ass."[159]

The donkey is the friend of man in his struggle to live with and transcend this earthly life. In "The Case of the Animals versus Man before the King of the Jinn," an Arabic epistle of the secret circa tenth-century philosophical society known as the Ikhwān al-Ṣafā' (The Brethren of Purity), the donkey jumps to his opponent's defense as the animals and the humans plead their case against one another. "Perfection belongs to God alone," he says, defending his flawed human rivals, turning the other cheek, and forgiving his oppressors with Christlike compassion. Nothing in creation is without lack, he argues, and as examples he cites the retrograde motions, eclipses, and flickering of the heavenly bodies. He does all this in service of the fallen creature that has enslaved and abused him for so long.[160]

As a faithful companion to mankind on his quest for spiritual advancement, the donkey figures prominently in religious literature, often serving as the mount of prophets and holy men. As will be shown in Section 4, the donkey speaks to his prophetic companion, and speaks in a startling voice – an alarm signaling the presence of the unseen. Or perhaps we should say "the unheard," for it may be the donkey's long ears and keen sense of hearing that lend him this power.[161] The donkey is not only a powerful speaker but a good listener whose ears serve as "intergalactic antennae."[162] His ability to perceive and give voice to hidden things renders him well suited to the needs of the prophets. And like his phallus, which contains a double significance, his voice is both earthly and uncanny, a sign of man's base nature as well as his potential to transcend.

4 The Voice of the Donkey

The donkey's far-reaching bray has frightened people for millennia.[163] He "alone among animals was not born in tune."[164] In contrast to his peaceful and stoic demeanor, these sudden vocal eruptions are startling and even uncanny, and thus have been taken as a sign of things hidden from the eyes of ordinary men. As we saw in Section 1, this was the sound that frightened the primordial giants of Greek myth. Musicologist Martin Vogel speculates that

159 Bruno, *The Cabala of Pegasus*, 20.

160 Ikhwān al-Ṣafā' / The Brethren of Purity, *The Case of the Animals versus Man before the King of the Jinn*, 64 (Arabic), 123–125 (English translation).

161 Ordine, *La Cabala Dell'Asino*, 13. Also see Vogel, *Onos Lyras*, 262 ff.

162 Merrifield, *The Wisdom of Donkeys*, 74. He is referring in part to the donkey's fabled ability to predict rain and other weather.

163 See Bough, *Donkey*, 74–75, which also highlights its comedic properties.

164 Aelian, *De Natura Animalium*, 10:28. Aelian attributes the information to Pythagoras and goes on to mention the popular "donkey with a lyre" trope discussed further later in this Element.

early donkey herders also used the bray to frighten their human enemies and concludes that their attempts to imitate the sound were responsible for the invention of basic musical instruments.[165] Tales of humans who imitate the donkey's bray for various purposes are found across great stretches of space and time. In some cases, donkey imitation can serve an apotropaic function, for just as the phallus wards off its mirror image (the evil eye), the imitation of the donkey's voice wards off the ill omen of its uncanny bray.

The underworldly connotations of the donkey's bray are ancient: one Egyptian text refers to hearing the voice of the "*hiw*-donkey" in the land of the dead.[166] A simultaneously ominous and apotropaic, double nature of the donkey's bray is also ancient,[167] since for the Egyptians, the bray was not only a frightening omen of evil, but the means of protection against evil: "the donkey's characteristics of being clamorous and strident relates to Seth's role in repelling the enemies of the Sun-god's solar barque from his position at the prow."[168] We hear the donkey's bray again in an enigmatic passage of the *Book of Dead*, in a speech apparently intended to confirm the departed person's innocence as their heart is weighed against a feather: "I am pure of mouth, pure of hands, one to whom 'Welcome!' is said at seeing him, because I have heard that speech said by the Donkey."[169]

This declaration has proven obscure to modern scholars, beyond confirming the "funerary/mortuary context" of the donkey and his strange voice.[170] It is clear, however, that underworldly associations with this vocalization persist through the centuries: the Christian theologian Jerome (d. 420) "Compares the braying of the ass to the singing of the devil."[171] The Qur'an, meanwhile, compares the bray to the hateful voice of the loud-mouthed boaster: "Nor strut about and stagger/ God has no love for boasters who swagger/ Be unassuming when you go on your way/And be soft when you have something to say – /For God, nothing is worse than a donkey's bray."[172] The two comparisons are not so different, because in the Qur'an, Satan's primary sin was arrogance; when God commanded him to bow down to Adam, he refused, boasting that "I am

---

165 He furthermore recounts several folk remedies designed to prevent a donkey from making this chilling noise (Vogel, *Onos Lyras*, 328–335).

166 Vandenbeusch, "Thinking and Writing Donkey," 142. She is referring to Coffin Text VII, spell 891, as found in Adriaan de Buck's edition.

167 This may also be perceived in the Zoroastrian creation myth, which says of the Three-Legged Donkey, "When it brays, all of Ohrmazd's female aquatic creatures become pregnant, but when the pregnant aquatic vermin hear that braying, they miscarry" (*Bundhisn*, book 24, verse 16). Ohrmazd or Ahura Mazda is the supreme creator deity.

168 Love, "Crum's Chicken," 678, which also describes the unlucky connotations of the sound.

169 Way, *Donkeys in the Biblical World*, 33 (Spell #125).

170 Way, *Donkeys in the Biblical World*, 34. We find a spell to summon the dead written on a donkey skin in the Greek Magical Papyri (Lucarelli, "The Donkey in Graeco-Egyptian Papyri," 97).

171 Van Schaik, *The Harp in the Middle Ages*, 127.

172 Qur'an 31:18–19, translated by Shawkat Toorawa.

better than him."[173] So, just as the phallus of the donkey represents man's base, lustful nature, his voice here represents man's Satanic arrogance. Because of the negative connotations of the bray in the Qur'an, in Islamic dream interpretation manuals, the voice of the donkey is an unlucky omen, as we will see.

A prophetic hadith pithily explains the ill-omened import of the donkey's voice, as well as the hidden matters it reveals:

> When you hear the rooster's cry, seek God's favour, for they have seen an angel. When you hear the donkey's bray, seek refuge with God from the devil, for they have seen a devil.[174]

It is no doubt due to this hadith that in twentieth-century Morocco (as anthropologist Westermarck claims), when a donkey is braying, it is perceived to be cursing its rider, or it is thought that Satan is "riding on its tail or blowing in its ear, or it sees the devil and wants to drive him away by cursing him."[175] It is interesting to note that in this final interpretation, the donkey's voice not only announces the presence of evil but repels it; the apotropaic potential of the bray is here present.

This prophetic hadith contrasts the harsh bray of the donkey with the crow of the rooster, whose voice announces the presence of angels.[176] Though the donkey's strident voice is not evocative of angels, we should note that there is some evidence, most famously the biblical story of Balaam, that donkeys can see not only devils but, like roosters, they see angels as well, and also announce their presence verbally. I will discuss this story in much more detail, but will only add here that the *Zohar* complicates this angel–devil dichotomy by claiming that Balaam, whose donkey saw an angel, "defiled himself nightly by mating with his donkey in order to draw upon himself the unholy spirit from the supernal serpent, thereby drawing on himself the spirit of unholiness. Then he cast his spells and enchantments ... until he drew to himself the spirits of defilement, who told him what he needed to know."[177] We can read this claim in relation to

173 Qur'an 7:12.

174 Al-Bukhārī, *Ṣaḥīh*, vol. 4, book 54, hadith 522. Also see al-Damīrī, *Ḥayāt al-ḥayawān al-kubrā*, 1:341. An extended version of this hadith includes the barking of dogs at night. "For indeed, they see what you do not see."

175 Westermarck, *Ritual and Belief in Morocco*, 2:287. Compare Bulliet's Arab-Israeli friend, Dr. As'ad Busool, whose village took a donkey braying at a funeral as a bad omen since it indicated that he had heard the screams of the damned in hell (*Hunters, Herder, and Hamburgers*, 154).

176 According to the earliest Persian commentaries on the Qur'an (as preserved in *Tafsīr-i Ṭabarī*), an angelic white rooster appeared to the prophet on his miraculous night journey to heaven (which, according to some versions, he undertook upon a steed that was half white donkey; see footnote 80). The cosmic white rooster is the symbol of the Zoroastrian angel Srōsh, and this association probably lies behind angelic rooster accounts in the Islamic tradition. See Zadeh, *The Vernacular Qur'an*, 319.

177 *Zohar*, 1.126a on www.sefaria.org/texts, a community translation project. Also see *Sanhedrin* 105a–b, which similarly accuses Balaam of sorcery and bestiality with a donkey (in the *William Davidson Talmud* on www.sefaria.org).

Section 3's argument, that sex with a donkey heralds the transformation of the body, leading to transcendence (in the case of Lucius), death (in the case of Rūmī's mistress character), or ritual defilement (here, in the case of Balaam). The donkey, like the rooster, is the usher to another level of reality, whether angelic or demonic.

The contrast between demonic donkey and angelic rooster becomes complicated and often collapses outright in medieval Arabic literature. For example, when the wine-loving poet Abū Nuwās (d. ca. 814) pleads "Pour wine for me until I see the rooster as a donkey!" he sets the two animals as opposites and then posits a mystical *coincidentia oppositorum* in the divine intoxication of his favorite drink.[178]

The donkey's voice can be contrasted with the rooster's because the donkey sees devils and the rooster sees angels; the donkey's voice is harsh and the rooster's is musical. But al-Jāḥiẓ, a contemporary of Abū Nuwās, suggests that donkeys could be substituted for roosters and used as alarm clocks[179] because both animals have an uncanny sense of time, suggesting knowledge of the unseen world:

> Were it not for the fact that the donkey is proverbial for his ignorance, were he to play the role of the rooster [braying] in the morning and the night, then that substitution and manner of proceeding would prove not unacceptable. For had one sought this service of the donkey, he would find him well organised, emitting a specific number of brays one after another, observable to be divided according to the hours of the night.
>
> And one may well have said then about the braying of the donkey, "He is not answering [another donkey], but rather they are both braying at the same time, each for the same reason,"[180] and the rooster, known for being better than an astrolabe, would have nothing over the donkey in this regard.
>
> The donkey's voice is farther reaching, however, and indeed the intensity of his voice led Aḥmad ibn 'Abd al-'Azīz to claim that the donkey never sleeps!
>
> "And why is that?" someone asked him.
>
> "Because," he said, "I find his scream sounds nothing like a notification of bedtime. It isn't the scream of someone who intends to go to sleep when he's done screaming!" . . . For this, the Qur'an rendered the donkey proverbial for his far-reaching voice as well as for his ignorance (when He said,

178 "*Asqinī ḥattā tarānī aḥsibu l-dīka ḥimārā*," Abū Nuwās, *Dīwān*, 165.

179 This is also the theme of a fable of La Fontaine titled "*L'Âne et ses Maitres*:" "*L'Âne d'un Jardinier se plaignait au Destin/ De ce qu'on le faisait lever devant l'aurore./ Les Coqs, lui disait-il, ont beau chanter matin;/ Je suis plus matineux encor.*" From *Les Fables de La Fontaine*, book 6, fable 11, 59–60, with thanks to Shawkat Toorawa for pointing this out.

180 These musings arise within the context of a larger discussion of the question of whether roosters crow at the same time because they are answering one another, or because they are both instinctually crowing at a specific time of day.

Figure 6 Episode 98 from Selove, *Popeye and Curly: 120 Days in Medieval Baghdad*, depicting the *coincidentia oppositorum* of donkey and rooster in the wine poetry of Abū Nuwās.

> "Like a donkey carrying tomes,"[181] for were there any kind of animal more ignorant of the contents of books than a donkey, God would have made a proverb about them instead).

As we saw in the Introduction, donkeys are associated with sleep-disturbing dreams and visions, and their raucous, ominous voice lies at the heart of this association. Their bray would certainly be as effective as a rooster's crow in jarring someone awake. In the Greek Magical Papyri, donkey bray and rooster crow are listed side by side as sounds that may jar someone out of a magically induced love trance.[182]

In daily life, the donkey has been used as a night watchman whose bray acts as a mundane burglar alarm.[183] But it also announces the presence of otherworldly things lurking in the dark. Perhaps it is for this that the *Book of Secrets*, attributed to Albertus Magnus, recommends the suffumigation of mixtures based on the "blood of an Ass congealed ... to see in our sleep what thing is to come of good and evil."[184] But shadowy things that loom in the night often turn out to be not demons, but frightening illusions, and the fact that the *Book of Secrets* also recommends the use of donkey hair and skin to produce such terrifying illusions shows that this contradictory beast is associated with false and misleading information as well as with hidden truths.[185]

---

[181] This verse, Qur'an 62:5, refers to recipients of divine revelation (such as the Torah) who recite the holy texts without living by their commandments.

[182] Lucarelli, "The Donkey in the Graeco-Egyptian Papyri," 99.

[183] Vogel, *Onos Lyras*, 327; Gregory, "Donkeys and the Equine Hierarchy," 194. Moreover, they are territorial and have sometimes been used as guard dogs (Donkey Sanctuary, "Factsheet: Owners and Guardians").

[184] Best and Brightman, *Book of Secrets*, 102.

[185] See Best and Brightman, *Book of Secrets*, 97–98, which, as mentioned in footnote 133, includes instructions for causing people to appear to have three heads, or the heads of asses. It furthermore provides instructions for causing nameless fear in children by use of a donkey skin (94).

Figure 7 An illustration from the thirteenth-century cosmography *Wonders of Creation*, surrounded by a text describing Satan, as well as the jinn who serve Solomon, and the various animal forms that they take. In this painting, we see a rooster-headed being on one side and a donkey (or perhaps mule)-headed being on the other. From *'Ajā'ib al-makhlūqāt wa-gharā'ib al-mawjūdāt* by Zakariyyā' ibn Muḥammad al-Qazwīnī, [fol. 99v] British Library, MS Or. 14140

Of course the more common association of donkeys with ignorance also appears in medieval grimoires: for example, the *Picatrix* recommends cultivating watermelon seeds in a donkey skull in order to cause people who consume these melons to grow foolish.[186] In al-Jāḥiẓ's argument, the uncanny reliability of the donkey's voice, which suggests that it knows hidden truths, is in contrast to its purported ignorance. We find this same conflict of ideas in the bestiaries of medieval Europe, which widely mock the donkey as stupid or lascivious but compare the regular cry of the wild ass at the vernal equinox to the manner in which monks mark time with their prayers. Thus, these bestiaries typically linked the wild ass (onager) with the devil; "paradoxically," writes Smithies, "the exception was when the onager represented the monk."[187] We might compare these monks marking sacred time to the claim in tractate Berakhot of the Babylonian Talmud that the heavenly night is divided into three watches, and the first transition between these watches is heralded on earth by the donkey's bray.[188] So, it seems that donkeys were widely perceived to bray at reliable times and this reliability had potentially spiritual import, suggesting that the donkey was privy to hidden information, and not as ignorant as he might superficially appear.[189]

As for al-Jāḥiẓ's claim about their ignorance, and the Qur'anic verse he cites in support of this claim (i.e., "donkeys carrying tomes"), this may suggest that they bear this wisdom without understanding it themselves. As previously mentioned, we can compare these tome-carrying donkeys to the Greek "*onos lyras*," and the medieval European donkey-with-a-lyre trope, of which Smithies writes, "like asses with lyres, unworthy students are incapable of understanding their textbooks."[190] The unmusicality of the donkey's voice further contributes to the comic effect of the trope: a braying donkey must make a poor musician. Likewise, it is funny to imagine a sleeper being jarred awake by their startling voice. But again, the comedic effect of al-Jāḥiẓ's argument and his conclusion that donkeys are ignorant are subtly undercut by the implication that their mysterious sense of time makes them a suitable alarm clock or even a caller to prayer. For we must bear in mind that in the Islamic world, rousing a sleeper to pray is among the alarm clock's most important functions.

In Islamic dream interpretation manuals, roosters, not donkeys, are the symbol of the caller to prayer (*muezzin*). For example, one popular manual advises that if you dream of becoming a rooster, you will become a *muezzin*; if you dream that a rooster enters your house and eats grain from the floor, you will be robbed by a *muezzin*![191] Dreams of donkeys do not evoke the caller to prayer. They are mostly signs of wealth and material comfort, while dreams of donkeys

---

186 Attrell and Porecca, *Picatrix*, 259. 187 Smithies, *Introducing the Medieval Ass*, 49.

188 *Barakhot*, 3a, in the *William Davidson Talmud* on www.sefaria.org.

189 Smithies, *Introducing the Medieval Ass*, 50.

190 Smithies, *Introducing the Medieval Ass*, 81. This is the trope from which Vogel derives the title of his book, *Onos Lyras*, and he addresses it especially on pages 354–359.

191 Nābulusī, *Ta'ṭīr al-anām*, 280.

braying are taken to be ill omens. Take, for example, this passage from Ibn Shāhīn's fifteenth-century *Al-Ishārāt fī 'ilm al-'ibārāt* (*Intimations on the Science of Interpretation*):

> Whosoever sees many donkeys, this indicates that his wealth and blessings will increase; it is better if the donkeys in the dream are obedient to their master.
>
> Dreams of donkey meat are visions of expanding commerce and wealth.
>
> Whosoever sees that he killed the donkey and ate of its flesh, this indicates that he should guard his money and live thriftily. And it is said, this indicates that he partook of forbidden goods . . .
>
> And it is said: There is nothing unluckier in dreams of the donkey than his voice, for the Almighty said this of it: "nothing is worse than a donkey's bray."[192]

An ancient Egyptian dream interpretation manual interprets dreams of eating donkey flesh as a sign that the dreamer will get a promotion.[193] We hear this echoed in Ibn Shāhīn's interpretation that "Dreams of donkey meat are visions of expanding commerce and wealth" – this despite the fact that donkey meat was not popularly consumed in ancient Egypt and was forbidden in Islam (which explains Ibn Shāhīn's alternate interpretation that such dreams indicate forbidden goods). The positive interpretation of the image stems partly from Egyptian wordplay that of course did not survive in the Arabic.[194] But it is also in tune with the donkey's wider interpretation as a good omen for material well-being. From the earliest point of our evidence, therefore, we might contrast the voice of the donkey with its body, or, more specifically, with its phallus, which, as I have shown, comes to represent the materiality of man's existence. This would explain why dreams of the donkey's physical presence and flesh are a sign of material prosperity, while its voice is an ill omen from the immaterial world, or the unseen. If this is so, the donkey phallus and the donkey tongue could be thought of as opposites, with one being a lucky or apotropaic sign of physical, material existence, and the other, an unlucky sign of hidden, otherworldly matters.

As is always the case with such oppositions, they become conflated or switch polarities with one another. This conflation of tongue with phallus will supply the theme of my Conclusion, but I will provide two somewhat facile examples here:

---

192 Ibn Shāhīn, *Al-Ishārāt*, 162–166. The final line refers to Qur'an 31:18–19 (Qur'an verse translated by Toorawa).

193 Vandenbeusch, "Thinking and Writing Donkey," 140. Also see Way, *Donkeys in the Biblical World*, 29–30. He furthermore addresses the symbol of donkeys in Akkadian dream interpretation manuals (90).

194 See Way, *Donkeys in the Biblical World*, 30, for the Egyptian wordplay. See Mavroudi, *Byzantine Book on Dream Interpretation*, for the influence of Egyptian dream interpretation on the medieval Islamic practice of the art (129).

in the European Middle Ages, the donkey's bray was thought to be a sign of lust, which connotation would explicitly link the phallus and the voice.[195] I previously drew a link between the comic garden god Priapus and the donkey's phallus as instrument of protection. In a tale in Ovid's *Fasti*, however, we see the voice of the donkey instead protecting against the attack of the phallus, when the donkey saves a sleeping nymph from being raped by the god: "But lo, Silenus' saddle-ass, with raucous weasand braying, gave out an ill-timed roar! The nymph in terror started up, pushed off Priapus."[196] Here the donkey's voice is lucky for the nymph and the phallus of Priapus is unlucky in that it is unwanted.

Thus do the phallus and the tongue stand as mirror image to one another, just as they each mirror themselves with their opposing symbolic resonances. For if the donkey's voice is generally unlucky, the donkey imitator must be lucky, according to the same logic whereby a mimetic image of the eye, or of the "one-eyed willy," can deflect the evil eye. Ḥamza al-Iṣfahānī's tenth-century study of "Arab superstitions" (*khurāfāt al-ʻarab*) claims that the desert-dwelling Arabs, upon entering a village afflicted with a pestilence, brayed ten times like a donkey in order to avert the illness.[197] There is even a word to describe this action: *taʻshīr* (from an etymological root related to the number ten), found in the more complete Arabic lexicons.[198]

---

[195] Smithies, *Introducing the Medieval Ass*, 98.

[196] Ovid, *Fasti*, 1.415. Later in *Fasti*, the myth is repeated, not with a nameless nymph, but with the virgin goddess Vesta (6.319). Ordine further links the donkey to Vesta in *La Cabala Dell'Asino*, 209n12.

[197] Mittwoch's edition (in *Abergläubische Vorstellungen*, 9–10) mentions that you must bray ten times, while that by Fahmī Sa'd (Ḥamza al-Iṣfahāni, *al-Amthāl*, 477) only mentions the braying and does not specify a number of times. Also see al-Damīrī, *Ḥayāt al-ḥayawān al-kubrā*, 1:358; al-Jābī, *Akhbār al-ḥamīr*, 101. Vogel, *Onos Lyras*, 331 links this apotropaic power to the bells that donkeys wear around their neck in ancient Roman art.

[198] Lane, *Arabic–English Lexicon*, 1:2050–1. This may also relate to much more ancient symbolic association of the donkey, for Mitchell writes that the Hittites used donkey figurines to figuratively carry (as a pack animal) pestilence and disease away from them and toward enemies (*The Donkey in Human History*, 99; cf. footnote 76). A translation of such a ritual is found in Beal, "Hittite Military Rituals." Way further describes the donkey as a "scapegoat" character in Hittite literature in *Donkeys in the Biblical World*, 72–73. Perhaps this is why Seligmann's *Die Zauberkraft des Auges und das Berufen* (1922) claims that "according to the ancient Arabs, the donkey was a holy animal and therefore immune from disease. Epidemics could not harm him" (404). He directs us to Smith's *Religion der Semiten* and Mittwoch's *Abergläubische Vorstellungen*. Donkeys are, however, obviously subject to disease, and potential victims of magical afflictions. Al-Malik al-Ashraf's veterinary manual prescribes a treatment for a mysterious form of water retention that afflicts donkeys and horses, which includes the incantation, "Oh, violent stomach-ache, get out of the beast belonging to so-and-so, son of so-and-so, unless he turns to believe in a god other than Allah!" Since, as Shehada notes in *Mamluks and Animals*, the veterinary manuals are mysteriously silent about the cause of this disease, we might surmise that a jinn or ill spirit could be to blame (212–213). And donkeys and other valuable beasts are often adorned with amulets that protect them from the evil eye; see Westermarck, *Ritual and Belief in Morocco*, 2:346.

It may be that Samson's weaponized jawbone of the ass also represents this apotropaic, reflective power of the donkey's voice.[199] Reflections of the donkey's voice, either through imitation, or through the talismanic object of the donkey jaw, would therefore function according to logic of symmetry or sympathy, according to Berlekame's theory of talismanic efficacy.[200] The two opposites of good and ill omen merge in their talismanic function.[201] And thus it is that the donkey, bearer of a voice of ill omen, and of the phallus that becomes a symbol of man's earthly body, also provides a suitable mount to the prophets. For their commonly perceived negative qualities of gross materiality and demonic noise contain their opposites in talismanic reflection. That is to say, phallus and voice also represent *transcendence* of the material and *protection* from the demonic.

Moreover, the donkey's ability to perceive what is hidden from man makes him a fit companion for prophets and holy men. Early depictions of the nativity, for example, sometimes show the donkey paying obeisance to the newborn messiah while his human companions remain oblivious to the sacred presence.[202] But the most famous example of a spiritually perceptive donkey is Balaam's jenny, who, in what initially seems like an asinine act of stubbornness, refuses to move forward on the path.[203] It is soon revealed, however, that she halted because she saw what her human rider could not: an angel of the Lord blocking their way – a sign of God's disapproval of their journey. When Balaam beats his donkey, she complains in human speech, making her the only animal to speak in the Bible except for the serpent of Eden.[204] Because of this biblical tale, the midrash (exegesis of the Hebrew scriptures) honored Balaam's ass as a miracle of nature "created between sunset and nightfall of the sixth day of creation."[205] *Lekach Tov*, an eleventh–twelfth-century commentary on the Torah, simply lists "the mouth of

199 See Bulliet, *Hunters, Herders, and Hamburgers*, 172. Bruno makes a similar argument in his *Cabala of Pegasus*, 24.

200 See Berlekame, "Symmetry, Sympathy, and Sensation."

201 This would explain the otherwise obscure interpretation of the Arabic saying "more disbelieving than an ass," as meaning that the donkey's "disbelief is actually a good omen for the blessedness of his owners" (Suliman Bashear, "Riding Beasts on Divine Missions," 58, referring to al-Zubaydī's *Tāj al-'Arūs* (an eighteenth-century dictionary), which also offers an alternative interpretation of the saying, suggesting that it refers to a specific man named Ḥimār (donkey).

202 Hobgood-Oster, *Holy Dogs and Asses*, 69.

203 Numbers 22:22. See Way, *Donkeys in the Biblical World*, 62 ff., 184 ff.

204 Smithies, *Introducing the Medieval Ass*, 45. She adds on page 48 that the ass was therefore associated in the minds of the medieval Christian commentators with Balaam as a false prophet, but since he was also associated with Jesus, this is another sign of his paradoxical/double status.

205 *Pesachim* 54a (in the *William Davidson Talmud*) lists Balaam's speaking donkey among ten miraculous phenomena that also includes the manna that fell from the desert. Also see Bulliet, *Hunters, Herders, and Hamburgers*, 171, and Alter, "Balaam and the Ass," 14.

the donkey" among these miracles.[206] We can now guess why one must insert one's head into the mouth of the donkey king, Abū Isrāʾīl, to learn his mysteries (as described in the Introduction): the donkey's mouth can be a gateway to the unseen and a miraculous sign from God.

The Lord himself speaks to Balaam in defense of his unjustly punished donkey, revealing that she had saved her rider's life. After the ass miraculously spoke, "the LORD unveiled Balaam's eyes, and he saw the LORD's messenger stationed in the road, his sword unsheathed in his hand, and he prostrated himself and bowed down on his face."[207] As Alter, translator and commentator of this passage points out, Balaam mimics the posture of the blessed donkey when bowing down, after learning from her the art of seeing the unseen. We are reminded of the erotic stories that we explored in Section 3, in which the donkey at once symbolizes the humiliation of the earthly body and the transcendence which follows this humiliation.

At least to modern ears, however, this biblical account still smacks of tragicomedy, and Alter argues that the comic resonance was audible even to ancient readers.[208] The spiritual donkey stands ever at the crossroads of holiness and satire, and it is not always clear in which light she should be interpreted. The Medieval European Feast of the Ass (Festum Asinorum), for example, is most typically interpreted as a "burlesque carnival," but it paid sincere homage to Balaam's miraculous ass as well as to the donkey who bore Jesus.[209] Smithies writes that the similar Feast of Fools (Festum Stultorum) used the ass to honor the humble nature of the subdeacon, who carried the holy communion bread and wine, just like the donkey carried Jesus. It was therefore a solemn ritual, which only "attracted censure" later.[210] But as for the Feast of the Ass, it was unlikely to have been a solemn occassion, if indeed "each part of the mass was accompanied by the comic braying, 'hinham!' [and] at the end of the service, instead of the usual blessing, the priest repeated the braying three times, and the final Amen was replaced by the same cry."[211]

The picture of mingled solemnity and humor around donkey speech abounds in medieval Arabic literature. In a tale of the early satirist Bashshār ibn Burd (d. ca. 784), he claims to have owned a donkey that recited poetry. After the donkey died, he appeared to his master in a dream and revealed in verse that he was slain

---

[206] *Midrash Lekach Tov*, commentary on Genesis 2.3.

[207] Translated by Alter, "Balaam and the Ass," 15. [208] Alter, "Balaam and the Ass."

[209] Smithies, *Introducing the Medieval Ass*, 58; Mitchell, *The Donkey in Human History*, 154; Bulliet, *Hunters, Herders, and Hamburgers*, 189.

[210] Smithies, *Introducing the Medieval Ass*, 146. She follows Max Harris's *Sacred Folly* in this reading.

[211] Bakthin, *Rabelais and His World*, 78, citing "a mass composed by the austere churchman Pierre Corbeille." Also see Vogel, *Onos Lyras*, 315–317.

by the love of a pretty jenny, whose cheek was smooth as a "shayqurān's." When Bashshār recited this poem to an audience, they asked for the definition of "shayqurān," and the poet replied, "It is one of the recondite words of the donkeys, so if you come across one, ask him."[212] Müller interprets this anecdote as a mixture of truth and fiction, with the dream being a work of fiction set within a historical account of the life of a poet.[213] Given his reputation as a joker, it is likely that Bashshār intended his invented dream to be funny first and foremost, but the note of tragedy, as well as the whiff of the supernatural, suit his asinine protagonist well.

In contrast to this levity, we find in al-Qushayrī's (d. 1072) collection of Sufi stories the tale of the holy man whose donkey spoke to him in human speech. The donkey's head was bowed under the attack of irritating flies, and when his master, Abū Sulaymān al-Khawwāṣ, swatted him with a stick to correct his behavior, the donkey turned to him and said, "Strike me, for thus shall you indeed be stricken." When his incredulous audience asks Abū Sulaymān if this really happened, he replied, "Just as you have heard it related."[214] Like Balaam, this donkey's rider was granted a divine correction for his bad behavior through the voice of his suffering mount. Moreover, the rider's ability to hear his donkey's message confirmed his status as a holy man.[215]

The prophet Muhammad himself spoke to his donkey, whose name, as mentioned earlier, was alternatively recorded as 'Ufayr or Ya'fūr. This donkey told the prophet about his previous owner and his own descent from a line of animals who had served former prophets.[216] The prophet would send Ya'fūr as a messenger to summon his companions.[217] This use of the donkey as a messenger is especially significant in light of the fact that, according to some reports, Solomon's messenger, a hoopoe bird, was also named Ya'fūr.[218] Solomon, of course, is the prophet most strongly associated with his ability to speak to animals, as well as with his knowledge of occult matters, facilitated by his conversation with his animal and jinn interlocutors. To assert a connection between the prophet's donkey and

[212] This last remark as translated by van Gelder in "Amphigory and Other Nonsense," 11. He and Müller provide a number of sources in which the anecdote can be found, but also see al-Jābī, *Akhbār al-ḥamīr*, 31.

[213] Müller, "Die Sprache des indischen Teufels," 332.

[214] Al-Damīrī, *Ḥayāt al-ḥayawān al-kubrā*, 1:357; al-Jābī, *Akhbār al-ḥamīr*, 41.

[215] Bashear, "Riding Beasts on a Divine Mission," 60n81, provides references to a range of reports in which talking animals confirm a prophet's status.

[216] Al-Damīrī, *Ḥayāt al-ḥayawān al-kubrā*, 1:357; Bashear, "Riding Beasts on a Divine Mission," 64.

[217] Bashear, "Riding Beasts on a Divine Mission," 64.

[218] Sindawi, "The Donkey of the Prophet," 96–97, refers us to two seventeenth-century collections of Shi'i hadith (al-Majlisī's *Biḥār al-Anwār* and al-Jazā'iri *Al-Nūr al-mubīn*). Also see al-Damīrī, *Ḥayāt al-ḥayawān al-kubrā*, 2:392.

Solomon's hoopoe further confirms the donkey's status as occult visionary and messenger of the unseen. Their symbolic relationship is bolstered by the fact that the hoopoe also carries ill-omened – and phallic – connotations of filth.[219] We might say that the hoopoe is a largely positive image with a negative shadow and the donkey is its symbolic mirror opposite.

We see Rūmī set the hoopoe and the donkey as opposites in his poem "Gazelle in the Donkey Stable."[220] The gazelle is tormented by its confinement in a stable with a donkey, and Rūmī describes this torment with a Qur'anic phrase, uttered by Solomon, who threatens to punish his absent hoopoe messenger "with a severe Penalty." It is a torment, a severe penalty, Rūmī explains, for the spirit as represented by the hoopoe/gazelle, to be confined in the ass-like body. The gazelle is the one of the most common symbols of beauty in Arabic and Persian love poetry, and here it represents the highest love of all, which is love of God. The donkey, as we have seen, represents all that is base and fallen about the human body and its desires, not to mention the demonic resonances of his bray. We can find the symbolic oppositions of gazelle and donkey echoed in magical practice, for gazelle skins are typically used as the material support for love spells, while donkey skin is used for spells of hatred.[221]

But as we have seen, the prophet's donkey, who performed the service of Solomon's hoopoe, transcended his fallen nature, refused to take a mate, and conveyed his thoughts to his master not with a harsh bray, but in human language. For this reason, he was permitted to perform the service of Solomon's hoopoe, his symbolic opposite, whom Rūmī compares to the gazelle. The prophet's messenger donkey, with Solomon's hoopoe's name, joined these oppositions in a single microcosmic being.

Our impulse may be to laugh at the thought of the donkey as divine messenger, for his comedic resonance is ever at odds with his prophetic associations. The two valences again combine into one in Cervantes's *Don Quixote,* where, as Smithies puts it, "Sancho and his ass were also Balaam-like. The all-seeing, all-knowing Sancho was contrasted with his metaphorically blind and irrational master."[222] I have elsewhere analyzed at length the tragi-comic tale of donkey voice imitation in Cervantes's work.[223] To summarize briefly, Don Quixote meets two men who

[219] Dupree, "An Interpretation of the Role of the Hoopoe," 173, 176.

[220] Rūmī, *Mathnawī*, book 5, poem 11.

[221] For donkey skin hatred spells, see the Introduction to this Element. For gazelle skin love spells, see Sakkākī, *Kitāb al-Shāmil* ("SOAS" manuscript 33a, 35b, 50a, and "Cairo" manuscript 95b, 134b, 135b, 136a–137a, 191b, 192b). We see these opposites strangely conjoined in al-Maʿarri's (d. 1057) *Risālat al-ṣāhil wa-l-shāḥij* (*The Epistle of the Horse and the Mule*), which includes a tale (told by an incredulous camel) about a gazelle in Basra who gave birth to a donkey. See Blankinship, "Al-Maʿarrī's Anxious Menagerie," 159 ff., for a discussion of the tale.

[222] Smithies, *Introducing the Medieval Ass*, 116.

[223] See our introduction to Al-Azdī, *The Portrait of Abū l-Qāsim*, 8–15.

are proud to discover that they are virtuosos at the art of donkey imitation, though this only earns them the mockery of their fellow villagers.[224] I have compared this tale to another striking donkey story, which similarly portrays both man's triumph and his absurdity, his admirable skill and his sheer foolishness, in the figure of a donkey impersonator: an anecdote in which al-Jāḥiẓ, with his characteristically serio-comic tone, recounts the uncanny ability of a donkey imitator to perfectly render the ideal donkey bray, rousing all the donkeys in the medieval Baghdadi neighborhood where he used to perform. Al-Jāḥiẓ uses this anecdote to prove that man is a microcosm who contains all opposites, "because he forms every form with his hand, and imitates every sound with his mouth, and because he eats plants like beasts of burden, and eats meat like beasts of prey, and eats seeds like birds, and because in him are the shapes of all the kinds of animals."[225]

This same argument is repeated in the *Picatrix*, which in describing man-as-microcosm, states, "There is no other animal with the ability to understand humans nor any that can change their voices and imitate others. The cock, the dog, and the lion, for example, cannot change their voices. Humans, with their own intrinsic voice, have the power of replicating the sounds of all the animals and of shaping their forms and likenesses as desired."[226] The idea that man is a microcosm is of course ancient and widespread, and fundamental to the practice of magic. In-depth explorations of this idea often assign specific animals, as well as celestial and geological phenomena, to specific parts of the human body and soul. The Ikhwān al-Ṣafā' (The Brethren of Purity), include several treatises that deal with the human microcosm in their collection of fifty-two epistles, which culminates in a treatise on magic. In their thirty-fourth epistle, they describe how the human body and soul is composed of the natures of minerals, plants, and animals.[227] Elaborating on the idea that there is a system of degrees (*martaba*) in the universe, reflected in the order of planets, they describe a hierarchy in the relation of plant to animal to man. For example, the highest of all plants, the date palm, resembles animals in that it bleeds and dies when decapitated, and has shallow roots that derive nutrients in a wormlike fashion.[228] Likewise the higher animals, like the monkey or ape, resemble man in the shape of his body, while the horse resembles man in his nobility and

[224] Cervantes, *Don Quixote*, book II, chapter 25.

[225] I have also discussed this anecdote at great length in previous publications and will refrain from repeating myself further here. See our introduction to Al-Azdī, *The Portrait of Abū l-Qāsim*, 8, and Selove, *Ḥikāyat Abī al-Qāsīm*, 71–72, 138–140, 148–149, 157.

[226] Attrell and Porreca, *Picatrix*, 64.

[227] They liken "mountains . . . to men's bones . . . rivers to intestines . . . cultural centers to the front of bodies, wilderness to the back." They drew parallels between "the wind and breathing . . . winter and old age [and] 'stars standing still' to stagnation in men's work" (Conger, *Theories of Macrocosms*, 49).

[228] Ikhwān al-Ṣafā', *Rasā'il*, 226.

perseverance. As for the donkey, he appears in similar microcosmic systems as a less noble version of the horse, or (as we might expect), as a representation of man's base and lustful nature.[229] As Rūmī describes it in the vivid donkey sex parable we explored in Section 3, the donkey is our bestial soul (*nafs bahīmī*), for God "will give our fleshly soul the form of an ass, because He makes the forms to be in accordance with the nature."[230]

We find the same cosmic hierarchy represented by animals and other beings in medieval Europe, specifically in William of Ockham's thirteenth-century *Opera Philosophica*. Humans have their place within this macrocosmic hierarchy, in which "an angel is more perfect than a human being, and a human being is more perfect than an ass."[231] The microcosm simultaneously exists in miniature within their form, and an individual human therefore reproduces this hierarchy within his or her own complex nature, which contains both angelic and asinine qualities.

In describing the *Opera Philosophica*'s position on the donkey, Smithies goes on to point out that Ockham ignored the animal's holy reputation and admirable work ethic, referring only to its asinine foolishness. And thus, perhaps, Ockham missed the donkey's own microcosmic qualities, as a symbol with stubbornly contradictory tendencies, unified into one mysterious being. As van Schaik puts it:

> The apparently contradictory opinions in medieval theology concerning the ass are bound up with the dualistic division of the cosmos into a positive half (directed towards God) and a negative half (directed towards the devil). Both the type and the antitype are formed in accordance with the same laws of existence. These laws allowed one and the same animal to be explained in a positive or a negative way, depending on the context.[232]

I would only add to this formulation that the opposites are reconciled in the figure of the donkey, who therefore represents not only a "dualistic division," but a *coincidentia oppositorum*, and a point at which the high and low are joined. As Bruno says, with his own deliberately contradictory blend of seriousness and jest, "it seems to me that [the donkey] is that World Soul itself, all in all, and everything in every part."[233] This is the source of the ass's power as an ingredient for the practice of magic.

---

229 Nokso-Koivisto, "Microcosm-Macrocosm Analogy," 93. This dissertation provides an excellent overview of the subject.

230 Rūmī, *Mathnawī*, vol. 5, line 1394.

231 Smithies, *Introducing the Medieval Ass*, 73, referring to William of Ockham's *Opera Philosophica IV.*

232 Van Schaik, *The Harp in the Middle Ages*, 129.

233 Bruno, *The Cabala of Pegasus*, 13: "*mi par che sia l'istessa anima del mondo, tutto in tutto, e tutto in qualsivoglia parte*," 97.

5 Conclusion

I have structured my argument around the symbolic dichotomy of voice and phallus. This dichotomy is strikingly painted in the following comic anecdote from al-Tawḥīdī's (d. 1023) *al-Baṣā'ir wa-l-dhakhā'ir* (*Insights and Treasures*):[234]

> A man said to Farazdaq, "I saw you in a dream being weighed against your donkey, and the donkey weighed more than you. Then the donkey's penis was cut off and placed in your ass, and you weighed more than the donkey. Then your tongue was cut off and placed in the ass of the donkey, and you weighed the same." "If your dream tells true," said Farazdaq, "I'll fuck your mother!"

Farazdaq (d. ca. 728) was a famous poetic satirist in the early days of Islam. It could be said that like all satirists, he had the power to curse his enemies with his sharp tongue, or to ward off the evil eye with a species of apotropaic "roasting."[235] This is more obviously the case because of his proximity to a pre-Islamic culture in which poets played an explicitly magical role. In light of this information, it seems that this prophetic dream plays with the complex connotations of the comic yet symbolically potent donkey and his various body parts.

I have drawn a contrast between the apotropaic donkey phallus (the *fascinum* that wards off evil) and the ill-omened donkey tongue (the bray when it sees Satan). We may also contrast the animal body of the human (represented by the donkey's phallus), enslaved to the base pleasures of the world, with man's transcendent mastery of symbols and signs (here represented by Farazdaq's tongue). For Farazdaq's insight as a poet gives him the ability to perceive, interpret, express, and manipulate the meanings hidden behind God's signs. In pre- and early Islamic culture particularly, the poet was regarded as a seer, a vessel of possessing jinn, and a practitioner of "halal sorcery."[236] In that light, Farazdaq's voice as a satirical poet is like the voice of the donkey, which also announces, however harshly, visions of the unseen. So we may depict Farazdaq as a donkey imitator and propose a potentially apotropaic quality of Farazdaq's obscene poetry. His tongue in that respect resembles the donkey's apotropaic penis, which mirrors the evil eye. We see

[234] Al-Jābī, *Akhbār al-ḥamīr*, 48.

[235] Elliot, "Magic and Satire: History," in *The Power of Satire*; Fahd, *La Divination Arabe*, 117. Barton, in *Sorrows of the Ancient Romans*, notes that "evil speech was often interchangeable, or conjoined in its effects, with the evil eye." It follows that a homeopathic remedy exists here too, for a verbal attack could both curse and heal. The scoffer/*derisor* is a regular fixture at royal courts and dinner parties, in order to provide the apotropaic variety of mockery. Conversely, flattery and praise are dangerous and suspect, they are "honey mixed with arsenic," thus necessitating the existence of ritualised, apotropaic verbal abuse (94, 108, 125–129, 142–3). I would argue that the same basic principals apply in sympotic literary settings in Medieval Arabic literature.

[236] See Selove, "Magic As Poetry," 38–40.

that a complex *coincidentia oppositorum* of tongue and phallus, man and beast, elevates this seemingly trivial tale.

We can work out the exact mathematical proportions of the tongue and the phallus here as well: it is a numerical constant for this balance to work. Farazdaq's tongue must weigh half as much as the donkey's penis, which in turn must weigh the amount of the original difference between them. So, if Farazdaq weighs eight stone, for example, and the donkey weighs ten stone, and the donkey's penis weighs two stone and Farazdaq's tongue weighs one stone, then you first subtract two from ten (put the donkey's penis in Farazdaq). Now Farazdaq weighs ten stone and the donkey eight. Then you subtract one from ten (put Farazdaq's tongue in the donkey) and they both weigh nine. The occult-minded reader may perceive a numero-lettrist vision of the universe here, for creation is a puzzle of numbers and signs, a *pons asinorum*, that only the wise may interpret.[237]

We must not overlook the fear of castration lurking behind this rather Freudian dream. By replacing the castrated phallus as Lacanian signifier, and the longing for meaning that it implies, with God, we may bring our theory a little closer to the thought world of the medieval Arabic literature from which this anecdote is derived.[238] Both in psychoanalytic theory and in the mystical Islamic (or Judeo-Christian) worldview, there is a feeling of being exiled from a paradisiacal wholeness, and in both cases, this is related to the sign as symbol of the Absent and the Unknown and expressed as a brokenhearted longing for the beloved. "Thus, in an esoteric context, the phallus, which in the Lacanian theory of signification is the structuring mark of desire, can be viewed as the signifier of esoteric knowledge."[239]

---

237 A *pons asinorum*, or asses' bridge, is a test or riddle that only the wise can decipher. It is also a Euclidian geometrical proof stating that "the base angles in an isosceles triangle are equal" (see Heilbron, "The Bridge of Asses"). It seems to me that the name is appropriate not only because this proof is a test for the unwise, but because it shows a balance between two opposite sides, which, as this Element has demonstrated, is an omnipresent feature of asinine symbology. We should note, however, that real-life donkeys are not fans of bridges: this is a trait Pliny the Elder observed in his first-century *Natural History* (8.68) and confirmed two millenia later by Andy Merrifield in *The Wisdom of Donkeys*, 84. Though as Merrifield observes, these are problems that man has foisted on the donkey, and are therefore human problems, not donkey problems (85). A popular Persian saying that translates as "the donkey has crossed that bridge" refers to a problem overcome that can now be safely forgotten (with thanks to Peyman Zinati for this information).

238 In a private communication to me, Daniel Beaumont clarifies the Lacanian point. "The mystic's Edenic wholeness is the womb. Lacan's talking about the infant immediately after birth which he sums up in his phrase 'the fragmented body.' The child before language experiences itself as a collection of uncoordinated parts. Only in the image of the other does he/she conceive itself as a whole." See his *Slave of Desire*, 32–33.

239 Tourage's *Rumi and the Hermeneutics of Eroticism* takes this observation as its starting point in analysing the fatal donkey sex poem discussed earlier (56, 68 ff.). He is relying here in part on Wolfson's Kabbalistic interpretation of the phallus in his "Occultation of the Feminine."

Faced with this Unknown, the choice is ours whether to make a Kierkegaardian leap of faith, and to believe even absurdly in the existence of a hidden Truth to which we might return.[240] I am reminded of Crowley's Devil card in his Thoth Tarot, which he likens not only to the "lilywhite goat . . . leaping with lust upon the summits of the earth" but to "the ass-headed god of the Egyptian deserts," and "the ass-headed idol of the Knights of the Temple" whom the "Early Christians . . . were accused of worshipping."[241] Wasserman interprets the card as indicating "aching discontent."[242] For me, this aching discontent, here symbolized by the devil, also stands for the longing of the human soul for reunion with the Divine. This is the physical urge that Rūmī's ill-fated mistress mistook for longing for simple sex.[243] As described in previous sections, some Sufi schools of thought depict Satan (Iblīs) as the ultimate monotheist, who would bow to none but his beloved creator, and who suffered, exiled, serving God's obscure purposes on earth while forever longing for their reunion.[244] The joining of these strange bedfellows – Crowley, Kierkegaard, and Rūmī – is enabled by the donkey who not only has Satanic and phallic associations but prophetic ones, and whose abject physical suffering shades into the Christlike.

That leaves us with the question of what Farazdaq's tongue is doing in the donkey's ass. Perhaps a Bakhtinian, carnivalesque renewal is implied. For the donkey is king of the carnival, or at least the carnival king's humble mount. He is the wise fool who makes us realize our own foolishness and thereby saves our souls. We must join the scholarly consensus in concluding that the donkey is a creature of inherent paradox. At once holy and profane, lucky and unlucky, ignorant and wise, the donkey straddles the line. One Arabic joke runs, "Which of these two donkeys is worse? That one and that one."[245]

We should also remember that behind this tangle of symbols stands a flesh-and-blood animal of extreme intelligence, kindness, and emotional depth. Real donkeys are not always well served by rumors of their magical or medicinal

---

[240] I refer here to Kierkegaard's *Fear and Trembling*, which tells the story of a hopeless lover who concludes:

> in one movement, more wonderful than anything else . . . "I nevertheless believe that I shall get her, namely on the strength of the absurd, on the strength of the fact that for God all things are possible." [For] only in the finite world [that] remains an impossibility. On this the knight of faith is just as clear: all that can save him is the absurd; and this he grasps by Faith. (75–76)

[241] Crowley, *The Book of Thoth*, 105–106.

[242] Wasserman, *Instructions for Aleister Crowley's THOTH Tarot Deck*, 12.

[243] Crowley expressed so many contradictory opinions about religion in his writings that it is difficult to gauge the level of discomfort he would feel in being included in this paragraph, but it is certain that he viewed sex as a path of union with the divine, and that his many influences included both Sufism and existentialism.

[244] This is the theme of Awn, *Satan's Tragedy*. [245] Al-Jābī, *Akhbār al-ḥamīr*, 104.

Figure 8 A photo of two donkeys, taken by the author at the Ivybridge Donkey Sanctuary

properties; "they have many symbolic burdens to overcome before they can be understood in their own right."[246] For example, "donkeys are being abused and slaughtered *en masse* for their skins, which are used in traditional Chinese medicine."[247] Moreover, the popular belief that they are stubborn may blind their owners to any reasonable objections a donkey may have to performing a task.[248] They have furthermore evolved the ability to hide their pain in order not to be perceived as weak by predators, and this allows humans to abuse them without seeing the suffering that they cause.[249] The assumption that they are unfeeling, stupid, or evil is therefore false and harmful to real donkeys.

[246] Bough, "The Mirror Has Two Faces." The article demonstrates that literary depictions of donkeys tend to portray them as allegories for the human condition rather than treat them as separate beings deserving of attention in their own right. Also see Gregory, "Donkeys in the Equine Hierarchy," 193–194.

[247] Desmond, "The Global Donkey Crisis: Yes, Really." It is tempting to see in the proposed purposes for the medicinal *ejiao* thereby produced, including "insomnia and reproductive issues," some of the symbolic associations we have explored in this Element with the donkeys and human sexuality, as well as with sleep and dreams. But this ancient remedy is said to cure a host of other illnesses as well, generally promoting blood circulation. See Kohle, "Feasting on Donkey Skin," 176–181. The Donkey Sanctuary proposes the use of cellular agriculture to artificially manufacture donkey collagen in order to meet demand for this product humanely and sustainably.

[248] "If a donkey is unsure of where they're being led, it will stop and consider the situation before proceeding. Some call this characteristic stubbornness or stupidity. We call this naturally analytical behaviour 'common sense'" (Donkey Sanctuary of Canada, "Donkey Myths"). As one donkey enthusiast puts it, "they have surprising reasoning abilities and must be shown not just how to do something, but why they should do it" (Miller, "12 Fascinating Things"). Also see Donkey Sanctuary, "Stubborn As a Donkey?" in "Knowledge and Advice."

[249] Donkey Sanctuary, *Clinical Companion of the Donkey*, 10.

They are in fact sensitive, empathetic, and emotionally intelligent beings. Volunteers at the Ivybridge Donkey Sanctuary confirmed what I have read in Pliny the Elder's *Natural History*: donkeys will mourn the death of their companions even to the detriment of their own health.[250] Their playful and cooperative nature renders them especially suitable as therapy animals. As the Donkey Sanctuary pamphlet "Donkey Assisted Activities: Guiding the Way to Wellbeing" puts it, "Donkeys are emotional, sentient animals who deserve our utmost care, respect, and understanding."

We may see in this same pamphlet, however, some echoes of donkeys' more esoteric symbolic associations – their ability, for example, to see the unseen: "As animals that have evolved to be highly sensitive to their environment, donkeys can read the emotional disposition of others around them, responding to factors we may not otherwise notice."[251] The donkey lovers who run this program and who have years of real-life experience with these animals unwittingly echo ancient philosophical ideas that man-as-microcosm might see himself reflected in this complex and paradoxical beast. "Donkeys provide the perfect mirror for humans to see their own internal emotional landscape," says one equine coach. "We celebrate the capacity for these sentient animals to teach us about ourselves and about our capacity for growth," the program manager confirms. Authors of medieval bestiaries, who wrote about animals so that man could learn about himself and God's creation, would probably concur.

Modern scholars of donkeys tend to lament the fact that their reputation has suffered to the point that the name of the donkey has become a slur or a curse and their sacred resonances have been forgotten.[252] But we should marvel at the power that the word "donkey" still holds, not only in modern English, but in languages around the world. How does uttering the name of a seemingly ordinary, lovable, common, and useful animal elicit immediate laughter or anger in the listener? You need only say "donkey" and you have made a powerful statement. It may be that the donkey himself has an emotionally affecting presence: "That's usually the case, more the rule, that passers-by smile, often smile, when you're walking with a donkey."[253] But this seems insufficient to explain the impact of their name. It can only be

[250] Pliny, *Natural History*, 8.68, states that they will mourn them even unto death, but the Donkey Sanctuary of course does not let things go that far. Also see Bekoff, "Donkeys: If they Aren't Grieving What Are they Doing?"

[251] Also see horsetalk.co.nz, "Equine Therapy: 'Zen-Like Grounded Quality' of Donkeys Helps Mental Health."

[252] Vogel, *Onos Lyras*, 16; Bulliet, *Hunters, Herders, and Hamburgers*, 190. Mitchell suggests that the donkey increasingly became a laughable beast – because it was used more and more by the poor and marginalized members of society as they were replaced by horses, camels, and mules for wealthier people (*The Donkey in Human History*, 229 ff.).

[253] Merrifield, *The Wisdom of Donkeys*, 66.

that the rich and ancient symbolic history of this animal is still alive in our modern minds, and that this long-accumulated symbolic weight still gives the word "donkey" the power to curse an enemy or to dispel the demons of fear with a laugh.

Scholars of asinine symbology love to cite theologian/detective novelist G. K. Chesterton's poem *The Donkey*, and I will here follow suit:[254]

> When fishes flew and forests walked
> And figs grew upon thorn,
> Some moment when the moon was blood
> Then surely I was born.
>
> With monstrous head and sickening cry
> And ears like errant wings,
> The devil's walking parody
> On all four-footed things.
>
> The tattered outlaw of the earth,
> Of ancient crooked will;
> Starve, scourge, deride me: I am dumb,
> I keep my secret still.
>
> Fools! For I also had my hour;
> One far fierce hour and sweet:
> There was a shout about my ears,
> And palms before my feet.

Chesterton was clearly well versed in his donkey lore, condensing so much of this animal's rich symbolism into his magical incantation of a poem: the donkey is a symbol of the topsy-turvy carnivalesque world with all its microcosmic mingling of terror and joy and its promise of transformation and renewal. This donkey is the trickster/holy man – an outcast, scourged and exiled like Satan, but also like Jesus, who rode his donkey to Jerusalem. And though we strive to peer into the depths of those asinine eyes, something remains hidden and mysterious in their stoic, uncanny, evocative gaze. "The ass, for his part, was as silent as could be."[255]

[254] Bulliet writes that this poem is "a rare sad reminder of a lost spiritual resonance" (*Hunters, Herders, and Hamburgers*, 172). Andy Merrifield addresses it in *The Wisdom of Donkeys*, 68 ff. This poem is also the epigraph to Bough's chapter "Donkeys in Literature, Film, and Art" in her *Donkey*, 129. She also uses it at the start of her article "The Mirror Has Two Faces." For a brief gloss, see Fambrough, "Chesterton's THE DONKEY."

[255] From the 1847 translation by Peter Motteux, Cervantes, *Don Quixote*, 114. Bough quotes this scene, depicting the touching reunion of Sancho with his donkey, in her "The Mirror Has Two Faces," 61.

At the end of Bruno's *Cabala of Pegasus*, the donkey pleads for entry into the academy – for recognition of his wisdom despite his tattered appearance. He is denied entry by a fool until the great god of the occult himself, Mercury/Hermes, takes up his cause and says "Since, ass, you hope to call yourself an academician, I, who have given you other gifts and favors, once again with complete authority ordain, constitute and confirm you universal academician and dogmatician, so you may enter and reside anywhere."

The vindicated ass turns to the fool who barred his way and asks, "Have you understood this?"

"We're not deaf," says the fool.[256]

Thus ends the *Cabala* and also this Element, which began by calling the donkey the party-crasher on the gravest of philosophical and theological studies. I urge my reader to keep an eye out for donkeys in your own intellectual pursuits, of whatever discipline and methodology, nor turn a deaf ear to this raucous plea: that they be admitted to your balanced consideration.

[256] Bruno, *The Cabala of Pegasus*, 90.

Bibliography

Abū Nuwās, *Dīwān*, volume 3, edited by Ewald Wagner (Beirut: Resalah, 2003).

Aelian, *De Natura Animalium/On the Characteristics of Animals*, volume 2, translated by Alwyn Faber Scholfield, Loeb Classical Library 448 (Cambridge, MA: Harvard University Press, 1959).

Agostini, Domenico, and Samuel Thrope (editors/translators), *The Bundahišn: The Zoroastrian Book of Creation* (New York: Oxford University Press, 2020).

Ahmed, Shahab, *What Is Islam? The Importance of Being Islamic* (Princeton, NJ: Princeton University Press, 2015).

Alter, Robert, "Balaam and the Ass," *Kenyon Review* 26:4 (2004): 6–7.

Apuleius, *Apuleius I Metamorphoseon Libri XI*, edited by Rudolf Helm (Leipzig: Teubner, 1955).

Attrell, Dan, and David Porreca (translators), *Picatrix: A Medieval Treatise on Astral Magic* (University Park: Pennsylvania University Press, 2019).

Augustine, Bishop of Hippo, *De civitate dei/The City of God against the Pagans*, edited and translated by R. W. Dyson (Cambridge: Cambridge University Press, 1998).

Awn, Peter, *Satan's Tragedy and Redemption: Iblīs in Sufi Psychology* (Leiden: Brill, 1983).

Al-Azdī, Abū l-Muṭahhar Muḥammad ibn Aḥmad, *The Portrait of Abū l-Qāsim al-Baghdādī al-Tamīmī*, edited and translated by Emily Selove and Geert Jan van Gelder (Harrow: H. A. R. Gibb Memorial Trust, 2021).

Bakhtin, Mikhail, *Rabelais and His World*, translated by Helene Iswolsky (Bloomington: Indiana University Press, 1984).

Barton, Carlin, *Sorrows of the Ancient Romans* (Princeton, NJ: Princeton University Press, 1992).

Bashear, Suliman, "Riding Beasts on Divine Missions: An Examination of the Ass and Camel Traditions," *Journal of Semitic Studies* 36:1 (1991): 37–75.

Bauer, Thomas, *A Culture of Ambiguity: An Alternative History of Islam*, translated by Hinrich Biesterfeldt and Tricia Tunstall (New York: Columbia University Press, 2021).

Beal, Richard H., "Hittite Military Rituals," in *Ancient Magic and Ritual Power* (Leiden: Brill, 2015).

Beaumont, Daniel, *Slave of Desire: Sex, Love, and Death in the 1001 Nights* (Vancouver: Fairleigh Dickinson University Press, 2002).

Bekoff, Marc, "Donkeys: If They Aren't Grieving What Are They Doing?" *Psychology Today*. https://bit.ly/46hSRAJ.

Berlekamp, Persis, "Symmetry, Sympathy, and Sensation: Talismanic Efficacy and Slippery Iconographies in Early 13th C Iraq, Syria, and Anatolia," *Representations* 133 (2016): 59–109.

Best, Michael R., and Frank H. Brightman (editors), *The Book of Secrets of Albertus Magnus of the Virtues of Herbs, Stones, and Certain Beasts; also A Book of the Marvels of the World* (Oxford: Oxford University Press, 1974).

Birant, Mehmet Ali, *Nasreddin Hodja* (Istanbul: AND Press, 1988).

Blankinship, Kevin, "Al-Maʿarrī's Anxious Menagerie: The Epistle of the Horse and the Mule," *Journal of Abbasid Studies* 8:1 (2021): 142–171.

Blood, H. Christian, "*Sed illae puellae*: Transgender Studies and Apuleius's *The Golden Ass*," *Helios* 46:2 (2019): 163–188.

Bough, Jill, *Donkey* (London: Reaktion Books, 2011).

"The Mirror Has Two Faces: Contradictory Reflections of Donkeys in Western Literature from Lucius to Balthazar," *Animals* 1:1 (2010): 56–68.

Bruno, Giordano, *The Cabala of Pegasus*, translated by Sidney L. Sondergard and Madison U. Sowell (New Haven, CT: Yale University Press, 2002).

Budge, E. A. Wallis, *Amulets and Magic* (London: Routledge, 2016).

Al-Bukhārī, Muḥammad, *Saḥīḥ al-Bukhārī*. https://sunnah.com/bukhari.

Bulliet, Richard, *Hunters, Herders, and Hamburgers: The Past and Future of Human–Animal Relationships* (New York: Columbia University Press, 2007).

The One-Donkey Solution: A Satire (Bloomington, IN: iUniverse, 2011).

Carus, Paul, "Anubis, Set, and Christ: The Significance of the 'Spottcrucifix," *Open Court* 15:537 (1901): 65–98.

Cervantes, Miguel de, *Don Quixote*, translated by Edith Grossman (New York: Harper Collins, 2005).

The History of Don Quixote de la Mancha, translated by Peter Anthony Matteux (London: James Burns, 1847).

Chu, Fran, Douglas E. Cowan, Brandon R. Grafius, et al., *Religion, Culture, and the Monstrous: Of Gods and Monsters* (Washington, DC: Lexington Books, 2021).

Conger, George, *Theories of Macrocosms and Microcosms in the History of Philosophy* (New York: Columbia University Press, 1922).

Crowley, Aleister (a.k.a. Master Therion), *The Book of Thoth: A Short Essay on the Tarot of the Egyptians, Being The Equinox Volume III No. V* (San Francisco: Weiser Books, reprinted 2017).

Dalal, Kurush F., Siddharth Kale, and Rajesh Poojari, "Four Gadhegals Discovered in District Raigad, Maharashtra," *Ancient Asia* 6:1 (2015): https://ancient-asia-journal.com.

Dallapiccola, Anna L., "Vāhanas," in Brill's *Encyclopedia of Hinduism Online*, edited by Knut A. Jacobsen, Helene Basu, Angelika Malinar, and Vasudha Narayanan, 2018. http://dx.doi.org.uoelibrary.idm.oclc.org/10.1163/2212-5019_BEH_COM_000348.

Al-Damīrī, Muḥammad ibn Mūsā, *Ḥayāt al-ḥayawān al-kubrā*, 2 volumes (Cairo: Muṣṭafā al-Bābī al-Ḥalabī, 1969–70).

DeFilippo, Joseph G., "Curiositas and the Platonism of Apuleius' *Golden Ass*," *American Journal of Philology* 111:4 (1990): 471–492.

Desmond, Jane. "The Global Donkey Crisis: Yes, Really." Scientific American Blog Network. *Scientific American*, 2020. https://blogs.scientificamerican.com/observations/the-global-donkey-crisis-yes-really.

The Donkey Sanctuary, *The Clinical Companion of the Donkey*, foreword by Professor James Duncan, edited by Linda Evans (Leicester: Matador, 2018).

"Donkey Assisted Activities: The Donkey Sanctuary." TheDonkeySanctuary.org.uk. www.thedonkeysanctuary.org.uk/about-us/donkey-assisted-activities.

"Keeping Donkeys with Other Animals: The Donkey Sanctuary." thedonkeysanctuary.org.uk, www.thedonkeysanctuary.org.uk/sites/uk/files/2020-04/keeping-donkeys-with-other-animals-factsheet-march-2020.pdf.

"Knowledge and Advice for Donkey Enthusiasts: The Donkey Sanctuary." www.thedonkeysanctuary.org.uk/what-we-do/knowledge-and-advice/for-owners/understanding-donkey-characteristics/stubborn-as-a-donkey.

Donkey Sanctuary of Canada, "Donkey Myths." www.thedonkeysanctuary.ca/information/donkey-myths.

Doostdar, Alireza, *The Iranian Metaphysicals: Explorations in Science, Islam, and the Uncanny* (Princeton, NJ: Princeton University Press, 2018).

Dupree, Nancy Hatch, "An Interpretation of the Role of the Hoopoe in Afghan Folklore and Magic," *Folklore* 85:3 (1974): 173–193.

Elliot, Robert, *The Power of Satire: Magic, Ritual, Art* (Princeton, NJ: Princeton University Press, 1960).

Fahd, Toufic, *La Divination Arabe: Etudes Religieuses, Sociologiques, et Folkloriques sur le Milieu Natif de l'Islam* (Leiden: Brill, 1966).

Fambrough, Preston, "Chesterton's THE DONKEY," *The Explicator* 63:1 (2004): 38–39.

Fancy, Nahyan, "Infertility in the Arabic Medical Commentaries, 1240–1520," presentation at University of Exeter, Premodern Fertility: Global Perspectives Workshop, May 25, 2022.

Frangoulidis, Stavros, *Witches, Isis and Narrative: Approaches to Magic in Apuleius' "Metamorphoses"* (Berlin: de Gruyter, 2008).

Frankel, Hans H., "*Onos Lyras: Der Esel mit der Leier*, by Martin Vogel" [Book Review], *Romance Philology* 29:1 (1975): 117–118.

Frankfurter, David, "The Perils of Love: Magic and Countermagic in Coptic Egypt," *Journal of the History of Sexuality* 10:3/4 (2001): 480–500.

Gordon, Stephen, "Al-Sakkaki's Grimoire and Medieval European Books of Ritual Magic," in *The Sorcerer's Handbook: Medieval Arabic Magic in Context* (Brill, forthcoming 2024).

Gregory, Justina, "Donkeys and the Equine Hierarchy in Archaic Greek Literature," *Classical Journal* 102:3 (2007): 193–212.

Grumach, Irene, "On the History of a Coptic Figura Magica," in *Proceedings of the Twelfth International Congress of Papyrology: Ann Arbor, Michigan, 13–17 August 1968*, edited by Deborah H. Samuel (Toronto: Hakkert, 1970), 172–173.

Guilhou, Nadine, "L'âne, portier de l'au-delà ou les métamorphoses," in *Apprivoiserle sauvage: Taming the Wild*, edited by M. Massiera et al. (Montpellier: Cahiers Egypte Nilotique et Mediterraneenne, 2015), 183–196.

Guillaume, Alfred, *The Life of Muhammad: A Translation of Ishaq's Sirat Rasul Allah*, thirteenth impression (Bangalore: Oxford University Press Pakistan, 1998).

Hammond, Marle, "From Phantasia to Paronomasia: Image-Evocation and the Double Entendre in Khalīl Ḥāwī's 'The Mariner and the Dervish,'" in *Takhyīl: The Imaginary in Classical Arabic Poetics*, edited by Geert Jan van Gelder and Marle Hammond (Oxford E. J. W. Gibb Memorial Trust, 2009), 274–286.

Hanfmann, George M. A., "The Donkey and the King," *Harvard Theological Review*, 78:3–4 (1985): 421–430.

Harris, Max, *Christ on a Donkey: Palm Sunday, Triumphal Entries, and Blasphemous Pageants* (Leeds: Arc Humanities Press, 2019).

Sacred Folly: A New History of the Feast of Fools (Ithaca, NY: Cornell University Press, 2011).

Heilbron, J. L., "The Bridge of Asses." *Encyclopedia Britannica*, 2001. www.britannica.com/science/The-Bridge-of-Asses.

Hobgood-Oster, Laura, *Holy Dogs and Asses* (Urbana: University of Illinois Press, 2008).

Horsetalk.co.nz. "Equine Therapy: 'Zen-like Grounded Quality' of Donkeys Helps Mental Health," 2018. www.horsetalk.co.nz/2018/10/12/equine-donkey-therapy-zen-mental-health.

Hyginus, *Astronomica Book Two, from The Myths of Hyginus*, translated and edited by Mary Grant (Lawrence: University of Kansas Publications in Humanistic Studies, 1960).

Ibn 'Arabī, Muḥyi l-Dīn [attributed], *Tafsīr al-Qur'ān al-karīm*, edited by Muṣṭafā Ghālib (Beirut: Dār al-Andalus, 1978).

Ibn Hishām, Abū Muḥammad 'Abd al-Mālik, *Al-Sīra al-Nabawiyya*, 4 volumes, edited by 'Umar 'Abd al-Salām Tadmurī (Beirut: Dār al-Kitāb al-'Arabī, 1987).

Ibn al-Jawzī, *Akhbār al-Ḥamqā wa-l-mughaffalīn* (Beirut: Dār al-Kitāb al-'Arabī, 2005).

Ibn Shāhīn, *Al-Ishārāt fī 'ilm al-ibārāt*, 2 volumes (Cairo: Muṣṭafā al-Bābī al-Ḥalabī, 1940).

Ikhwān al-Ṣafā' / The Brethren of Purity, *The Case of the Animals versus Man before the King of the Jinn: An Arabic Critical Edition and English Translation of Epistle 22 /al-Risālah al-thāminah min al-qism al-thānī fī l-ṭabī'iyyāt: fī aṣnāf al-ḥayawānāt wa-'ajā'ib hayākilihā wa-gharā'ib aḥwālih*, edited and translated by Lenn E. Goodman and Richard McGregor (Oxford: Oxford University Press / Institute of Ismaili Studies, 2009).

Rasā'il ikhwān al-ṣafā' (Beirut: Dar Sader, 1957).

Al-Iṣfāhānī, Ḥamza, *Sawā'ir al-amthāl 'alā af'al*, edited by Fahmi Sa'd (Beirut: 'Ālam al-Kutub, 1988).

Al-Jābī, Bassām 'Abd al-Wahhāb, *Akhbār al-ḥamīr fī al-adab al-'arabī* (Beirut: Dar ibn Ḥazm, 2002).

Jacobi, Renate, "The 'Khayāl' Motif in Early Arabic Poetry," *Oriens* 32 (1990): 50–64.

Al-Jāḥiẓ, Abū 'Uthmān 'Amr ibn Baḥr, *al-Bayān wa-l-tabyīn*, edited by 'Abd al-Salām Muḥammad Hārūn, 4 volumes (Cairo: Maktabat al-Khānjī, 1968).

al-Ḥayawān, edited by 'Abd al-Salām Muḥammad Hārūn, 8 volumes (Cairo: Muṣṭafā al-Bābī al-Ḥalabī, 1965–9).

Johnston, Sarah Iles, "Defining the Dreadful: Remarks on the Greek Child-Killing Demon," in *Ancient Magic and Ritual Power*, edited by Marvin Meyer and Paul Mirecki (Leiden: Brill, 1995), 361–387.

Josephus, Flavius, *Against Apion* in *The Works of Flavius Josephus*, translated by William Whiston (Auburn, NY: John E. Beardsley, 1895).

Jung, Carl, "On the Psychology of the Trickster-Figure," in *The Archetypes and the Collective Unconscious* (Princeton, NJ: Princeton University Press, 1969): 255–274.

Kierkegaard, Soren, *Fear and Trembling*, translated with an introduction by Alastair Hannay (London: Penguin Books, 1985, reprinted 2003).

Koehle, Natalie, "Feasting on Donkey Skin," in *Conspicuous Consumption*; edited by C. A. Smith, N. Kohle, and L. Jaivin (Canberra: ANU Press, 2018).

Krappe, Alexander, "Apollon Onos," Classical Philology 42 (1947): 223–234.

Kristó-Nagy, István T., "A Violent, Irrational, and Unjust God: Antique and Medieval Criticism of Jehovah and Allāh," in *La Morale au crible des religions, Studia Arabica, XXI*, edited by Marie-Thérèse Urvoy (Versailles: Editions de Paris: 2013): 143–164.

Lactantius, *Institutiones Divinae/Divine Institutes*, translated by William Fletcher in *Ante-Nicene Fathers*, volume 7, edited by Alexander Roberts, James Donaldson, and A. Cleveland Coxe (Buffalo, NY: Christian Literature Publishing, 1886): 77–81.

La Fontaine, Jean de, *Les Fables de Jean de la Fontaine, Livres 5–8* (Montreal: La Bibliothèque électronique du Québec, n.d.).

Lane, Edward, *Arabic–English Lexicon*, 2 volumes (Cambridge: Islamic Texts Society, reprinted 1984).

Lazarus Yafeh, Hava, "ʿUzayr," in *Encyclopaedia of Islam, Second Edition*, edited by P. Bearman et al. Brill Reference Online. July 14, 2023. http://dx.doi.org/10.1163/1573-3912_islam_SIM_7787.

Leck, Ralph, "Westermarck's Morocco: Sexology and the Epistemic Politics of Cultural Anthropology and Sexual Science," in *Global History of Sexual Science, 1880–1960*, edited by Veronika Fuechtner, Douglas E. Haynes, and Ryan M. Jones (Oakland: California Scholarship Online, 2018): https://doi.org/10.1525/j.ctt1vjqqxw.

Litwa, David M, *The Evil Creator: Origins of an Early Christian Idea* (New York: Oxford University Press, 2021).

Love, Edward O. D., "'Crum's Chicken': Alpak, Demonised Donkeys, and Avianised Demons among the Figures of Demotic, Greek, and Coptic Magical Texts," in *Magikon zōon: Animal et magie dans l'Antiquité et au Moyen Âge*, edited by Jean-Charles Coulon (Paris: Institut de recherche et d'histoire des textes, 2022): 661–726.

Lucarelli, Rita, "The Donkey in the Graeco-Egyptian Papyri," in *Languages, Objects, and the Transmission of the Rituals: An Interdisciplinary Analysis on Ritual Practices in the Graeco-Egyptian Papyri (PGM)*, edited by Sabina Crippa and Emanuele M. Ciampini (Venice: Edizioni Ca'Foscari, 2017): 89–104.

Lucian, *Soloecista, Lucius or The Ass, Amores, Halcyon, Demosthenes, Podagra, Ocypus, Cyniscus, Philopatris, Charidemus, Nero*, translated by M.D. MacLeod. Loeb Classical Library 432 (Harvard, MA: Harvard University Press, 1967).

Al-Maʿarrī, Abū l-ʿAlāʾ, *Risālat al-ṣāhil wa-l-shāḥij*, edited by ʿĀʾisha ʿAbd al-Raḥmān "Bint al-Shāṭiʾ" (Cairo: Dār al-Maʿārif, 1975, reprinted 1984).

Mackay, Christopher S. (translator), *The Hammer of Witches: A Complete Translation of the* Malleus Maleficarum (Cambridge: Cambridge University Press, 2010).

Marashi, Taryn, "More Than Beast: Muhammad's She-Mule Duldul and Her Role in Early Islamic History," *International Journal of Middle East Studies* 53:4 (2021): 639–54.

Mason, Hugh, "Greek and Latin Versions of the Ass-Story," *Aufstieg und Niedergang der Roemischem Welt* 2:34.2 (1994): 1666–1707.

Mavroudi, Maria, *A Byzantine Book on Dream Interpretation: The* Oneirocriticon of Achmet *and Its Arabic Sources* (Leiden: Brill, 2002).

McCown, Chester Charlton (editor), *The Testament of Solomon* (Leipzig: J. C. Hinrichs, 1922).

de Menasce, Jean, *Une Apologétique mazdéenne du XIe siècle: Škand-gumānīk vičār, la solution décisive des doutes* (Fribourg: Librairie de l'Université, 1945).

Merrifield, Andy. *The Wisdom of Donkeys: Finding Tranquility in a Chaotic World*. New York: Bloomsbury, 2010.

Miller, Marcy J., "12 Fascinating Things You Never Knew about Donkeys," PetHelpful, 2019. https://pethelpful.com/farm-pets/Twelve-Fascinating-Things-You-Never-Knew-about-Donkeys.

Mitchell, Peter, *The Donkey in Human History: An Archaeological Perspective* (Oxford: Oxford University Press, 2018).

Mittwoch, von Eugen, *Abergläubische Vorstellungen und Bräuche der Alten Araber Nach Ḥamza al-Isbahānī* (Berlin: Reichsdruckerei, 1913).

Müller, Kathrin, "Die Sprache des indischen Teufels. Anekdoten zwischen sprachlicher Realität und Fiktion," in *Story-Telling in the Framework of Non-fictional Arabic Literature*, edited by Stefan Leder (Wiesbaden: Harrassowitz): 309–344.

Nābulusī, ʻAbd al-Ghanī ibn Ismāʻīl, *Taʻṭīr al-anām fī taʻbīr al-manām*, edited by Yūsuf al-Shaykh Muḥammad (Beirut: al-Maktabah al-ʻAṣrīyah, 1997).

Al-Nafzāwī, Muhammad ibn Muhammad, *Al-Rawḍ al-ʻāṭir fī nuzhat al-khāṭir*, edited by Jamāl Jumʻa (London: Riyāḍ al-Rayyis li-l-Kutub wa-l-Nashr, 1993).

Nasr, Seyyed Hossein et al., *The Study Quran: A New Translation and Commentary* (New York: Harper Collins, 2015).

Nokso-Koivisto, Inka, "Microcosm-Macrocosm Analogy in Rasā'il Ikhwān aṣ-Ṣafā' and Certain Related Texts," doctoral dissertation, University of Helsinki, 2014.

Novetzke, Christian Lee, "Traces of a Medieval Public," in *The Quotidian Revolution Vernacularization, Religion, and the Premodern Public Sphere in India* (New York: Columbia University Press, 2016): 74–102.

Ockenström, Lauri, "The Deviance of Toz: The Reception of Toz Graecus and Magical Works Attributed to Toz in the 12th and 13th Centuries," in *Esotericism and Deviance*, edited by Manon Hedenborg White and Tim Rudbøg (Leiden: Brill, forthcoming 2023).

Ogden, Daniel, *Magic, Witchcraft and Ghosts in the Greek and Roman Worlds: A Sourcebook*, second edition (Oxford: Oxford University Press, 2009).

Ordine, Nuccio, *La Cabala Dell'Asino: Asinita e Conoscenza Giordano Bruno* (Naples: Liguori Editore, 1996).

Giordano Bruno and the Philosophy of the Ass, translated by Henryk Barański and Arielle Saiber (New Haven, CT: Yale University Press, 1996).

Overman, Arundell (editor), *The Illustrated Goetia: Lesser Key of Solomon* (Independently Published, 2020).

Ovid. *Fasti*, translated by James G. Frazer, revised by G. P. Goold. Loeb Classical Library 253 (Cambridge, MA: Harvard University Press, 1931).

Paret, R., "al-Burāḳ," in *Encyclopaedia of Islam, Second Edition*, edited by P. Bearman, et al., 2012. http://dx.doi.org.uoelibrary.idm.oclc.org/10.1163/1573-3912_islam_SIM_1527.

Pliny, *Naturalis historia/Natural History, Volume I: Books 1–2*, translated by H. Rackham. Loeb Classical Library 330 (Cambridge, MA: Harvard University Press, 1938).

Plutarch, "Isis and Osiris," in *Moralia*, vol. 5, translated by Frank Cole Babbitt. Loeb Classical Library 306 (Cambridge, MA: Harvard University Press, 1936).

Qazwīnī, Zakarīyā ibn Muḥammad, *Ajā'ib al-makhlūqāt wa-gharā'ib al-mawjūdāt*, British Library: Oriental Manuscripts, Or 14140, in Qatar Digital Library. www.qdl.qa/archive/81055/vdc_100023630151.0x0000c7.

Richlin, Amy, *The Garden of Priapus: Sexuality and Aggression in Roman Humor*, second edition (New York: Oxford University Press, 1992).

Ridpath, Ian, *Star Tales* (London: Lutterworth Press, 2018).

Riggs, Christina, *Ancient Egyptian Magic: A Hands-On Guide* (London: Thames and Hudson, 2020).

Rūmī, Jalāl al-Dīn, *Mathnawī = The Mathnawí of Jalálu'ddín Rúmí*, five volumes, edited and translated by Reynold A. Nicholson (London: Luzac, 1925–40).

Saif, Liana, "The Cows and the Bees: Arabic Sources and Parallels for Pseudo-Plato's Liber Vaccae." *Journal of the Warburg and Courtauld Institutes* 79:1 (2016): 1–47.

"From Ghāyat al-Hakīm to Shams al-Maʿārif: Ways of Knowing and Paths of Power in Medieval Islam," Arabica 64:3–4 (2017): 297–345.

"A Preliminary Study of the Pseudo-Aristotelian Hermetica: Texts, Context, and Doctrines," *Al-ʿUṣūr al-Wusṭā* 29 (2021): 20–80.

Al-Sakkākī, Sirāj al-Dīn, *Kitāb al-Shāmil wa-baḥr al-kāmil* (Cairo: Dār al-Kutub al-Miṣriyyah, now available as a microfiche in Dubai: Juma al-Majid Cultural Centre, ms. 1735).

Kitāb al-shāmil wa-baḥr al-kāmil (London: School of Oriental and African Studies, MS 46347).

Schlam, Carl C., *The "Metamorphoses" of Apuleius: On Making an Ass of Oneself* (Chapel Hill: University of North Carolina Press Enduring Editions, 2009).

Seligmann, Siegfried, *Die Zauberkraft des Auges und das Berufen* (Hamburg: Friederichsen, 1922).

Selove, Emily, "A Dream Theory of Translation," in *The Sorcerer's Handbook: Medieval Arabic Magic in Context* (Brill, forthcoming 2024).

Ḥikāyat Abī al-Qāsīm: A Literary Banquet (Edinburgh: Edinburgh University Press, 2016).

"Magic As Poetry, Poetry As Magic: A Fragment of Arabic Spells," *Journal of Magic, Ritual, and Witchcraft* 15:1 (2020): 33–57.

Popeye and Curly: 120 Days in Medieval Baghdad (Fargo, ND: Theran Press, 2021).

Seybold, John, "The Earliest Demon Lover: The *Ṭayf al-Khayāl* in *al-Mufaḍḍalīyāt*," in *Reorientations/Arabic and Persian Poetry*, edited by Suzanne Pinckney Stetkevych (Bloomington: Indiana University Press, 1994): 180–189.

Shehada, Housni Alkhateeb, *Mamluks and Animals: Veterinary Medicine in Medieval Islam* (Leiden: Brill, 2012).

Silvia de Leon-Jones, Karen, *Giordano Bruno and the Kabbalah: Prophets, Magicians, and Rabbis* (New Haven, CT: Yale University Press, 1997).

Simpson, Jacqueline, and Steve Roud (editors), "Sin-Eating," in *A Dictionary of English Folklore* (Oxford: Oxford University Press 2003). https://bit.ly/3ELVdMA.

Sindawi, Khalid, "The Donkey of the Prophet in the Shiʿite Tradition," *Al-Masaq*, 18:1 (2006): 87–98.

Smith, Morton, *Jesus the Magician* (New York: Harper and Row, 1978).

Smith, William Robertson, *Lectures on the Religions of the Semites* (Edinburgh: Adam and Charles Black, 1889).

Smithies, Kathryn, *Introducing the Medieval Ass* (Cardiff: University of Wales Press, 2020).

Steinsaltz, Rabbi Adin (translator), *William Davidson Talmud* (Korenpublishers), Sefaria.org.

Tacitus, *Complete Works of Tacitus*, translated by Alfred John Church, William Jackson Brodribb, and Sara Bryant (New York: Random House, 1873, reprinted 1942).

Al-Tawḥīdī, Abū Ḥayyān ʿAlī ibn Muḥammad ibn al-ʿAbbās, *al-Baṣāʾir wa-l-dhakhāʾir*, 9 volumes, edited by Wadād al-Qāḍī (Beirut: Dār Ṣādir, 1988).

Tobias, Michael, and Jane Morrison, *Donkey: The Mystique of Equus Asinus* (San Francisco: Council Oak Books, 2006).

Todd, Evelyn T., Laure Tonasso-Calvière, Loreleï Chauvey, et al. "The Genomic History and Global Expansion of Domestic Donkeys," *Science* 377 (2022): 1172–1180.

Toorawa, Shawkat, "A Translation of Q Luqmān/31," in *His Pen and Ink Are a Powerful Mirror: Andalusi, Judaeo-Arabic, and Other Near Eastern Studies in Honor of Ross Brann*, edited by Adam Bursi, S. J. Pearce, and Hamza M. Zafer (Leiden: Brill, 2020): 326–328.

Tourage, Mahdi, *Rūmī and the Hermeneutics of Eroticism* (Leiden: Brill, 2007).

Turner, Philip, "Seth: A Misrepresented God in the Ancient Egyptian Pantheon?" [Thesis]. Manchester, UK: University of Manchester, 2012.

Vandenbeusch, Marie, "Thinking and Writing 'Donkey' in Ancient Egypt: Examples from the Religious Literature," *Altorientalische Forschungen* 46:1 (2019): 135–146.

Van Gelder, Geert Jan, "Amphigory and Other Nonsense in Classical Arabic Literature," in *Ruse and Wit: The Humorous in Arabic, Persian, and Turkish Narrative*, edited by Dominic Parviz Brookshaw (Boston: Ilex Foundation 2012): 7–32.

"The Lamp and Its Mirror Image: Hâzim al-Qartâjannî's Poetry in the Light of His Path of the Eloquent and Lamp of the Lettered," in *Takhyīl: the Imaginary in Classical Arabic Poetics*, edited by Geert Jan van Gelder and Marle Hammond (Oxford: E. J. W. Gibb Memorial Trust, 2009): 265–273.

Van Schaik, Martin, *The Harp in the Middle Ages: The Symbolism of a Musical Instrument* (Leiden: Brill, 2021).

Vogel, Martin, *Onos lyras: Der Esel mit der Leier* (Dusseldorf: Gesellschaft zur Forderung der Systematischen Musikwissenschaft, 1973).

Ward, William A., "The Hiw-Ass, the Hiw-Serpent, and the God Seth," *Journal of Near Eastern Studies* 37:1 (1978): 23–34.

Wasserman, James, *Instructions for Aleister Crowley's THOTH Tarot Deck* (York Beach: Samuel Weiser, 1983).

Way, Kenneth, *Donkeys in the Biblical World: Ceremony and Symbol* (University Park: Pennsylvania State University Press, 2011).

Westermarck, Edward, *Ritual and Belief in Morocco*, 2 volumes (London: Macmillan, 1926).

Wheeler, Brannon M., *Animal Sacrifices and the Origins of Islam* (Cambridge: Cambridge University Press, 2022).

Wirkud, Harshada, "Study of Gadhegals in Maharashtra: A Holistic Approach to the Study of Gadhegals," in *Essays in Honour of Prof Arvind P Jamkhedkar, The Proceedings of the Workshop on Explorations in Maharashtra*, edited by Kurush F. Dalal (Mumbai: India Study Centre Trust, 2017): 48–62.

Wolfson, Elliot R., "Occultation of the Feminine and the Body of Secrecy in Medieval Kabbalah," in *Elliot R. Wolfson: Poetic Thinking*, edited by Hava Tirosh-Samuelson and Aaron W. Hughes (Leiden: Brill, 2015): 35–68.

Ye, Qing, "Reading Bodies: Aesthetics, Gender, and Family in the Eighteenth-Century Chinese Novel *Guwangyan* (*Preposterous Words*)" Doctoral Dissertation, University of Oregon, 2016.

Zadeh, Travis, *The Vernacular Qur'an: Translation and the Rise of Persian Exegesis* (Oxford: Oxford University Press, 2012).

El-Zein, Amira, *Islam, Arabs, and the Intelligent World of the Jinn* (Syracuse, NY: Syracuse University Press, 2009).

Acknowledgments

For such a short Element, I have many people to thank, not all listed by name here; so many of my friends and colleagues have patiently suffered my talking about donkeys at far greater length than is typically considered polite. Daniel Beaumont read a complete draft of this work and offered his advice and encouragement. Mohammed Sanad joined me in a minute analysis not only of the *Book of the Complete*'s ritual to summon the donkey king, but of the seven nights' worth of lengthy Arabic invocations to follow. Rob Gleave and his Centre for the Study of Islam at the University of Exeter offered further comments on this corrupt and difficult text and smiled politely as I talked about the phallus. Other members of this Centre, especially Omar Anchassi and István Kristó-Nagy, followed up by sending me further materials to consider, and Sajjad Rizvi calmly answered years of philosophical questions about donkeys. Members of Exeter's Centre for Magic and Esotericism were similarly helpful, especially Siam Bhayro, Catherine Rider, Marion Gibson, and Daniel Ogden. Arghavan Moharrami helped me read the Persian poem by Rūmī which features so prominently in this Element. Richard Bulliet shared some of his own superior work on donkeys by email. Many friends who knew of my interests sent material my way, which allowed me to shape my argument, including Geert Jan van Gelder, Amy Richlin, Shawkat Toorawa, Nicholas Banner, Bryar Bajalan, Travis Zadeh, Matthew Melvin-Koushki, and my own mother. The Leverhulme Trust funded my research into the donkey king himself. Finally, I would like to thank my students, especially on my module ARA2001: From Holy Text to Sex Manuals (whose secret title for those in the know is "From Holy Text to Donkey Sex"). For the errors that I have doubtlessly committed, I have only my own asininity to thank.

This book is dedicated to Eeyore, former resident of the Ivybridge Donkey Sanctuary.

Cambridge Elements

Magic

Marion Gibson

University of Exeter

Marion Gibson is Professor of Renaissance and Magical Literatures and Director of the Flexible Combined Honours Programme at the University of Exeter. Her publications include *Possession, Puritanism and Print: Darrell, Harsnett, Shakespeare and the Elizabethan Exorcism Controversy* (2006), *Witchcraft Myths in American Culture* (2007), *Imagining the Pagan Past: Gods and Goddesses in Literature and History since the Dark Ages* (2013), *The Arden Shakespeare Dictionary of Shakespeare's Demonology* (with Jo Esra, 2014), *Rediscovering Renaissance Witchcraft* (2017) and *Witchcraft: The Basics* (2018). Her new book, *The Witches of St Osyth: Persecution, Murder and Betrayal in Elizabethan England*, will be published by CUP in 2022.

About the Series

Elements in Magic aims to restore the study of magic, broadly defined, to a central place within culture: one which it occupied for many centuries before being set apart by changing discourses of rationality and meaning. Understood as a continuing and potent force within global civilisation, magical thinking is imaginatively approached here as a cluster of activities, attitudes, beliefs and motivations which include topics such as alchemy, astrology, divination, exorcism, the fantastical, folklore, haunting, supernatural creatures, necromancy, ritual, spirit possession and witchcraft.

Cambridge Elements

Magic

Elements in the Series

A full series listing is available at: www.cambridge.org/EMGI

Printed in the United States
by Baker & Taylor Publisher Services